THER!

NAVY

FIRST IN   ALWAYS
THE FIGHT-   FAITHFUL-
BE A U.S. MARINE!

JOIN THE
AIR SERVICE
and
SERVE
in
FRANCE

DO IT
NOW

I WANT YOU
FO

With German prisoners of war (left) and American soldiers everywhere, the traffic to and from Mont St. Pere on July 23, 1918, is in a state of chaos, as the Allied counteroffensive drives a spearhead in the Marne salient.

COVER: *Lieutenant Douglas Campbell in his Nieuport 28 prepares to shoot down the German Rumpler that has been firing on him but is now out of ammunition.*

FRONT ENDSHEET: *Posters came into their own as powerful weapons in World War I.*

CONTENTS PAGE: *Howard Chandler Christy painted this poster for a bond drive.*

BACK ENDSHEET: *Old songs and magazines recall World War I and the Jazz Age.*

*"A knowledge of the past prepares us for the crisis
of the present and the challenge of the future."*

JOHN F. KENNEDY
From his special foreword in Volume I

THE AMERICAN HERITAGE
NEW ILLUSTRATED HISTORY
OF THE UNITED STATES

VOLUME 13

WORLD WAR I
AND THE TWENTIES

By ROBERT G. ATHEARN
Professor of History, University of Colorado

CREATED AND DESIGNED BY THE EDITORS OF
AMERICAN HERITAGE
The Magazine of History

PUBLISHED BY
DELL PUBLISHING CO., INC., NEW YORK

CONTENTS OF THE COMPLETE SERIES

Foreword by JOHN F. KENNEDY
Introduction by ALLAN NEVINS
Main text by ROBERT G. ATHEARN

A MASTER INDEX FOR ALL 16 VOLUMES APPEARS IN VOLUME 16

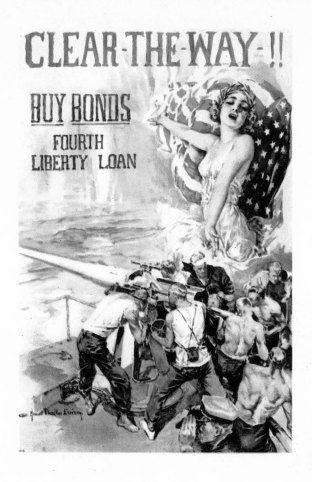

CONTENTS OF VOLUME 13

CHAPTER 37

THE GREAT CRUSADE

A little more than a year after Woodrow Wilson's inauguration, an event took place in Europe that was not only to destroy the uneasy peace there, but eventually to involve an isolationist America in a conflict from which it would emerge the leading power in the world. The nations of Europe were split into two major groups, between which a balance of power existed. On one side was the Triple Entente—France, Great Britain, and Russia; on the other, the Triple Alliance—Germany, Austria-Hungary, and (until 1915) Italy—also called the Central Powers. On June 28, 1914, Archduke Francis Ferdinand of Austria, heir to the throne of aged Emperor Francis Joseph, was assassinated at Sarajevo by a Serbian nationalist. At first, it appeared that this Balkan crisis might simmer down, but a month later, Austria severed relations with Serbia, a move that preceded war by only a few days. Germany backed Austria; Russia stepped forward to defend its small Balkan friend; and despite all efforts by would-be peacemakers to localize the dispute, France, Belgium, and soon Great Britain were involved. Almost overnight, Europe was at war.

American relations with European nations were at that time generally friendly, especially with Great Britain. But Wilson quickly called upon his countrymen to take no sides and to be "impartial in thought as well as action." The suggestion, admired as a theory, was largely ignored by the man on the street. Millions of "hyphenated" Americans—German-Americans, Irish-Americans, and others of foreign extraction—remembered the old country and had the normal sympathies toward their respective homelands. Even the governments abroad did not believe that Wilson would long honor his own words. Sir Cecil Spring-Rice, British ambassador to the United States, remarked that he was sure Wilson had "an understanding heart." The diplomat was right. Even though Wilson stated his desire for neutrality in a public declaration on August 19, 1914,

Woodrow Wilson is the archetype of the idealist whose most cherished plans are frustrated by the realities of politics. Sir William Orpen painted him in 1919.

The assassination of Austrian Archduke Francis Ferdinand in June, 1914, caused a Balkan crisis that grew into World War I.

the American government soon began to show sympathy for the Allies (as the Entente governments came to be called) in their struggle against the Central Powers.

Friendship and neutrality are hard to combine in wartime. British complaints against alleged German breaches of international law made matters particularly difficult for Wilson. There was sharp pressure from private banking firms for permission to loan money to the Allies. Officially,

Wilson frowned upon the practice, but before the year 1914 was out, the City Bank of New York had loaned the French government $10,000,000. When peace-minded Congressmen expressed a desire to create an arms embargo, thus shutting off supplies to the Allies, the administration repudiated the idea. Meanwhile, American farmers and manufacturers protested any restrictions on international trade. Cotton farmers saw an opportunity to capitalize upon the war and overcome a downward trend in prices. The South, a Democratic stronghold, had to be considered. In short, Wilson the idealist once again found himself confronted with realities and was obliged to retreat before the barrage of economic demands. Before long, his administration had to take the position that Americans could sell goods or loan money to any foreign country. It was a concession filled with risks, and Wilson knew it.

As the war went on, American involvement deepened. Walter Hines Page, United States ambassador to London, was outspoken in his belief that America should enter the war against Germany. When Wilson tried to tone him down, Page became uncooperative to the point of giving the British information he should have kept secret. The ambassador's attitude, supported by expressions of friendship from other Americans, encouraged the British to believe they could push their control of the world's shipping lanes even to the point of

"All the News That's Fit to Print."

The New York Times.

THE WEATHER
Fair today and Sunday, fresh to strong southwest to west winds.
For full weather report see Page 3.

VOL. LXIV...NO. 20,923. ··   NEW YORK, SATURDAY, MAY 8, 1915.—TWENTY-FOUR PAGES.   ONE CENT In Greater New York, Jersey City and Newark. | Elsewhere TWO CENTS.

LUSITANIA SUNK BY A SUBMARINE, PROBABLY 1,000 DEAD; TWICE TORPEDOED OFF IRISH COAST; SINKS IN 15 MINUTES; AMERICANS ABOARD INCLUDED VANDERBILT AND FROHMAN; WASHINGTON BELIEVES THAT A GRAVE CRISIS IS AT HAND

SHOCKS THE PRESIDENT

Washington Deeply Stirred by Disaster and Fears a Crisis.

BULLETINS AT WHITE HOUSE

Wilson Reads Them Closely, but Is Silent on the Nation's Course.

HINTS OF CONGRESS CALL

Loss of Lusitania Recalls Firm Tone of Our First Warning to Germany.

CAPITAL FULL OF RUMORS

Reports That Liner Was to be Sunk Were Heard Before Actual News Came.

Special to The New York Times.

WASHINGTON, May 7.—Never since that April day, three years ago, when word came that the Titanic had gone down, has Washington been so stirred as it is tonight over the sinking of the Lusitania. The early reports told that there had been no loss of life, but the relief that these advices carried gave way to the greatest concern late this evening when it became known that there had been many deaths. Although they are profoundly reticent, officials realize that this tragedy, involving the loss of American citizens, is likely to bring about a crisis in the international relations of the United States.

It is pointed out that the sinking of the Lusitania is the outcome of a series of incidents that have been the

The Lost Cunard Steamship Lusitania
X Where the First Torpedo Struck.   XX Where the Second Torpedo Struck.

SOME DEAD TAKEN ASHORE

Several Hundred Survivors at Queenstown and Kinsale.

STEWARD TELLS OF DISASTER

One Torpedo Crashes Into the Doomed Liner's Bow, Another Into the Engine Room.

SHIP LISTS OVER TO PORT

Makes It Impossible to Lower Many Boats, So Hundreds Must Have Gone Down.

ATTACKED IN BROAD DAY

Passengers at Luncheon—Warning Had Been Given by Germans Before the Ship Left New York.

LONDON, Saturday, May 8.—The Cunard liner Lusitania, which sailed out of New York last Saturday with 1,918 souls aboard, lies at the bottom of the ocean off the Irish coast.

She was sunk by a German submarine, which sent two torpedoes crashing into her side at 2:30 o'clock yesterday afternoon while the passengers, seemingly confident that the great, swift vessel could elude the German underwater craft, were having luncheon.

The great inrush of water caused the liner to list heavily to port, so that she could not launch many of her lifeboats

Cunard Office Here Besieged for News; Fate of 1,918 on Lusitania Long in Doubt
Fate of Most of the Well-Known Passengers Still in Doubt —Story of Disaster Long Unconfirmed While Anxious Crowds Seek Details.

Roosevelt Calls It Piracy; Says That We Must Act.
Special to The New York Times.
SYRACUSE, N. Y., May 7.—Ex-President Roosevelt, after learning details of the

Meagre List of Saved Received in New York
Those whose rescue was reported to New York by Cable by the Liverpool offices of the Cunard Line and

Loss of the Lusitania Fills London With Horror and Utter Amazement
News Held Back for Hours—Anxious Crowds Wait All Night at Steamship Offices for Word of Friends and Relatives.

The New York Times *stated that the* Lusitania *had been "twice torpedoed" on May 7, 1915. It was hit only once; then an internal explosion followed.*

stepping on neutral toes. Attempting to cope with the growing dilemma, Wilson talked at length with his closest adviser, Colonel Edward M. House. He read to the colonel from *The History of the American* by Professor Woodrow Wilson, pointing out that the War of 1812 had grown from a similar situation. Historian Wilson remarked that he and James Madison were the only two Princeton men to become President, and that the circumstances they faced in international war had, so far, run parallel. This was as far as he wanted the comparison to go; he had to avoid involvement.

The Germans, too, objected to British methods. On February 4, 1915, they proclaimed the waters around the British Isles a war zone and said they would sink all enemy ships found there. Also, they told neutrals to stay away, as the British were guilty of misusing a neutral flag to disguise their own ships. Germany had a point. Colonel House, while traveling on the

U-boats sank many British vessels in their tightened blockade of the islands in early 1917, crippling Britain's shipping and threatening the country with starvation.

British liner *Lusitania* in February, 1915, was surprised to see the American flag run up as the vessel approached the Irish coast. When the United States remonstrated, the British argued that the Germans ought to stop any ships whose identity they doubted. Both sides knew this was impractical, as German submarines, or U-boats, would not surface and risk being shot out of the water by a deck gun. Nonetheless, Wilson protested the submarine blockade of the British Isles and warned against the sinking of any American ships.

In a desperate war, the neutral always runs a heavy risk. It was true in the Napoleonic Wars and it was true in Wilson's day. On March 28, 1915, the first American life was lost in the sinking of the British ship *Falaba*. A month later, German airplanes attacked the American steamship *Cushing,* and on May 1, the American tanker *Gulflight* was torpedoed. That same day, the *Lusitania* sailed from New York carrying American passengers who had ignored the German embassy's warnings. A week later, as she approached the Irish coast, the *Lusitania* was topedoed and sunk with the loss of 1,198 lives, including 128 Americans. From New York to San Francisco the press condemned this "slaughter," "wholesale murder," and "piracy" by the Ger-

mans. Colonel House predicted we would be at war within a month.

Despite a German apology, and the revelation that the *Lusitania* carried military supplies and 4,200 cases of cartridges, the incident had a profound effect on both the American people and the administration. Continued sinkings kept public anger high. In the spring of 1916, the French steamer *Sussex* was torpedoed, injuring some of her American passengers. As

Germany had agreed not to sink unarmed passenger vessels without warning, Wilson got from the Germans what he regarded as a promise to modify their conduct. This *"Sussex pledge"* was to be used as a test of Germany's sincerity. For nine months it was kept.

Apparently satisfied, Wilson ran for re-election in 1916, with "He kept us out of war" as his supporters' best slogan. Although Charles Evans Hughes, the Republican candidate, made it a close race, Wilson won. The following January, Germany again tightened its blockade on the British Isles and announced it would sink all suspicious ships. Wilson regarded the renewal of unrestricted submarine warfare as a violation of the *Sussex* pledge. His desire to be neutral was further weakened when, late in February, he learned that the German foreign secretary,

THE NAVY NEEDS YOU! DON'T READ AMERICAN HISTORY— MAKE IT!

U·S·NAVY RECRUITING STATION
34 E. 23rd St., N.Y. & 23 N. Broadway, Yonkers, N.Y.

This recruiting poster hoped to make white-collar stay-at-homes eager for adventure.

Alfred Zimmermann, had cabled his minister at Mexico City to make an alliance with Mexico in case of war with America. The minister was to promise the Mexicans the return of New Mexico, Arizona, and Texas and was to try to persuade the Mexican president to invite the Japanese into the alliance. Zimmermann's note, intercepted by British intelligence, was turned over to Ambassador Page, who sent it to the State Department. News of the Zimmermann proposal was released to the public in March,

the same month that three American ships were attacked without warning and sunk. Wilson decided to ask Congress to recognize that a state of war existed between the United States and Germany. On April 6, 1917, the resolution had passed both houses. Wilson signed it, and America's neutrality ended. Wilson the peaceful, Wilson the idealist was now a war President.

A democracy goes to war

If America were going to fight a total war, every bit of available manpower would have to be tapped. Men had volunteered in greater numbers than the army could use during the Spanish-American War, but the present conflict was different. Not only was the enemy far away and much more formidable, but young men were no longer so eager for glory. For several years they had read of mud and blood in the trenches of France, and they found little glamour in the idea of fighting against tanks, machine guns, and poison gas.

Clearly the volunteer system would not work. The answer was conscription, which would provide not only the necessary manpower but would allow the government to draw on it in an equitable manner. Knowing the traditional American antipathy toward the draft, and remembering the bitter riots it had caused during the Civil War, Wilson tried to minimize the complaints he knew would come. Thus the government arranged that young men be inducted by boards

1090

*American destroyers arrived at Queenstown, Ireland, in May, 1917, to help
hunt down German submarines that were fast cutting off transport to England.*

made up of people from their own communities.

Quietly the administration prepared its conscription bill, and on May 18, 1917, it became law—although Speaker of the House Champ Clark claimed there was "precious little difference between conscript and convict." On June 5, more than 9,000,000 men, between the ages of 21 and 30, registered for service.

In the prewar years, Wilson had been criticized for his failure to prepare the country for possible involve-ment. Now his administration pushed mobilization with every resource at its command. Army camps began to dot the land, and civilian contractors fought with one another for lumber, steel, plumbing supplies, and all other materials necessary to build them. Food, bedding, clothing, and innumerable additional requirements for an army of several million had to be procured, and ships had to be built to carry them across the ocean.

America also had to produce new weapons, for the advances in armaments since 1914 had outmoded much of the equipment already owned by the army and navy. There was such a shortage in artillery, and what existed was so antiquated, that for heavy ordnance America would rely chiefly upon guns supplied by the French and British. There was no national aircraft industry. When the United States went to war, its air arm (then part of the army) had but 55 airplanes, all of them obsolete; most American pilots flew in craft either designed or built by the Allies.

"Over there"

The apparent indifference of the Germans to America's entry into the war represented a gamble. Although well aware of the potential power of the newest belligerent, the planners at Berlin were confident that their U-boats could starve out the British Isles before the slow-moving trans-atlantic democracy could get an army in the field.

It was a great risk, but in 1917 the odds seemed to be in their favor. From January to June, submarines sank 2,275,000 tons of British shipping and 1,580,000 tons of Allied and neutral shipping. Both sides knew that if this rate increased, the Allies would be in serious difficulty, for ships could not be built as fast as they were being sunk. The only hope the Allies had was to improve their antisubmarine methods. In the second half of 1917,

Surrounded by rubble, a doughboy stands over the body of a dead comrade and fires at the enemy in Harvey Dunn's painting of street combat in France.

the use of convoys and depth charges cut shipping losses almost in half, and in the early months of 1918, it appeared that the Germans had miscalculated their ability to isolate the British Isles.

A second miscalculation was the belief that America would be slow in mobilizing her tremendous resources. Not only was a Selective Service Act passed within a few weeks after Wilson signed the war resolution, but Congress also quickly enacted legislation authorizing two Liberty Loan drives and soldiers' and sailors' insurance; controlling aviation, food, and fuel; increasing taxes; setting more severe punishment for espionage; and forbidding trading with the enemy. By October, appropriations totaling almost $19,000,-000,000 had been approved. For the Allies, however, America's war effort was all too slow. Not until October was any of the American Expeditionary Force at the front, and then only token detachments stationed in quiet sectors. By the end of 1917, perhaps 250,000 American servicemen were in France, most of them still in advanced training. General John J. Pershing, commander in chief of the A.E.F., asked for 1,000,000 men in France by the end of May, 1918, but by March had only 500,000.

Even more distressing to the Allies was the quarrel with the American military over how the expeditionary force would be used. Pershing insisted upon a separate American

SMITHSONIAN INSTITUTION

General John J. "Black Jack" Pershing, commander in chief of the American Expeditionary Force in Europe, refused to integrate his divisions with other Allied troops.

army; the French and British wanted to integrate the newly arrived troops with their own as quickly as possible. Pershing was deaf to pleas that Germany might win before his troops got into action, and that as both American officers and men were untested in battle, it was unwise to entrust a whole sector of the front to inexperienced divisions. The argument grew so acrimonious that England's Prime Minister David Lloyd George and French Premier Georges Clemenceau went over Pershing's head and appealed to Woodrow Wilson. But the President stood firmly behind his general.

The early months of 1918 marked the high point of the war for Germany. A revolution-torn Russia had been beaten decisively, and in March, 1918, the new Bolshevik leaders gave in to the harsh terms imposed by the Germans in the Treaty of Brest-Litovsk, thus ending the war on the eastern front. Freed from this commitment, and now able to transfer vast numbers of men to the west, the Germans prepared a mighty series of offensives aimed at crushing the British and French before the Americans arrived.

On March 21, 1918, three German armies numbering well over 800,000 men struck the British along a 40-mile front, and within two days, British Field Marshal Douglas Haig's outnumbered troops were in full retreat. As the British swung back toward the Channel, ready to evacuate by sea, they opened a gap between themselves and the French forces. But before the Germans could exploit it, the French sent reinforcements, and the Allied line held. During the spring of 1918, the Germans continued to hammer at the Allied defenses. Again and again they made spectacular gains, only to be stopped short of a truly decisive victory. By summer, however, great numbers of Americans were ready to fight, and it became apparent that the German gamble had failed.

In mid-July, the German commander, Erich von Ludendorff, made his final effort, launching an attack in the Marne Valley aimed at Paris. This struggle was the turning point of the war—for here the exhausted Germans were halted once and for all, and an Allied counteroffensive began. Now there were 1,000,000 Americans in France, and another 500,000 would arrive before November. Using American troops to spearhead the drive in the Marne salient, the Allies pushed the German armies back; soon a general attack was mounted all along the western front. Although the Germans put up a stiff resistance, their fight was hopeless. By fall, with their armies in collapse and revolution threatening at home, they willingly agreed to an armistice. Thus, on November 11, 1918, World War I came to an end.

If American aid was late, it came when most needed. It boosted Allied morale when at its lowest ebb. In an almost continuous series of battles, American troops captured nearly 45,-000 prisoners, took some 1,400 guns, and brought down over 700 enemy aircraft. Over 50,000 Americans died in battle, a slight figure compared to the losses of the Allies, who had been fighting more than four years. Active American participation had lasted no more than a few months.

The home front

At home, noncombatants made their contribution, too. In mobilizing civilians, Wilson had three able assistants—Newton D. Baker, Secretary of War; Bernard M. Baruch, chairman of the War Industries Board; and George Creel, head of the Committee on Public Information. Creel and Baruch were performing tasks with-

The air full of poison gas, the Marine Brigade of the Second Division at the Battle of Belleau Wood fights through its grim 19-day engagement.

out precedent in American history, and their orders were often criticized.

Baruch had the problem of running all American industry as if it were a single factory. For example, the War Industries Board decided that 8,000 tons of steel a year was too much to allot to women's corsets, and it stopped the manufacture of them. Then, to avoid hurting a civilian industry, the board let corset manufacturers make masks and belts for the Army Medical Corps. So it was in other industries. Women's blouse factories made signal flags, radiator manufacturers made guns, automobile factories

Tanks manned by American soldiers slowly make their way up a hill to go into battle with the Germans near Bourevilles, France, on September 26, 1918.

made airplane engines, and piano companies made airplane wings.

Labor was a key segment of the civilian army. Wages of industrial workers rose so fast that inflation resulted, causing a wave of potentially crippling strikes by the fall of 1917. Workers rightly claimed that their real wages were diminishing as prices went up. To stop the spiral, the government formed the National War Labor Board, with ex-President Taft and labor lawyer Frank Walsh at its head. Companies flouting its decisions were taken over by the government. And when workers became unreasonable, they were threatened with induction into the armed services, a device that was usually effective.

Although the government was obliged to take over some industries as a punitive measure, it did so with others for greater efficiency. In December, 1917, the government assumed control of all major railroads, under the ex-Secretary of the Treasury, William G. McAdoo. The railroads complained that their rolling stock was being mishandled or allowed to deteriorate, that government concessions to labor would make postwar labor-management problems more difficult, and that federal operation would decrease the general efficiency of the lines, but their outcries were lost in the general din of mobilization.

As always in wartime, there were shortages. To make the maximum use of fuel, so necessary to manufacturers and military alike, a fuel administrator was appointed. Marshal Ferdinand Foch of France issued a grim warning to the United States: "If you don't keep up your oil supply, we shall lose the war." But in a day when natural gas was not available in quantity across the land, coal was just as important to both homes and factories, and with the demands of the war, it was becoming increasingly

The chaos of war is everywhere on a road at Esnes, France, on September 29, 1918, as American troops push their way to the front in the Meuse-Argonne offensive.

scarce. As a crisis mounted in the winter of 1917–18, Fuel Administrator Harry A. Garfield, former president of Williams College, ordered that industrial plants east of the Mississippi River be shut down on Mondays until the end of March. Offices, stores, schools, and places of amusement also had their coal supply sharply curtailed. Civilians were asked to observe "heatless Monday" and to "save a shovelful of coal a day." To save gasoline and oil, they were urged to do less pleasure driving by observing "gasless Sunday."

An administration to conserve food was set up, headed by Herbert Hoover. As European demand for foodstuffs increased, Americans had to tighten their belts; as Wilson put it, they were "now eating at a common table." The Allies particularly needed fats and sugar. To aid them, Americans sharply reduced their own use of sugar and pork, while farmers made every effort to raise more pigs. As one commentator wrote, "The American hog became an exalted animal, commanding for the moment a rather more intent regard than the lion or the eagle; the hog population was almost as much a concern to the government as manpower."

Finally, a huge propaganda campaign was mounted on the home front. George Creel's Committee on Public Information employed any and all who could transmit ideas—singers, painters, sculptors, illustrators, designers, and cartoonists. The country was literally plastered with posters— in streetcars, on billboards, on barn walls, along highways, and in all public buildings. Volunteer "Four-Minute Men" stood up in lodge meetings, dining clubs, schools, union meetings, and even in lumber camps to give their brief but urgent message. Tin Pan Alley did its share also, producing *Over There, Goodbye Broadway,*

As in all war propaganda, the enemy in 1918 became the symbol of everything that was ruthless, destructive, and horrifying.

Hello France, and a host of other tuneful reminders that a world war was in progress.

By November 11, 1918, it was, as George M. Cohan's popular song said, "over, over there." A little more than three weeks later, the American liner *George Washington* sailed for Europe carrying President Wilson. The former college professor broke a tradition, for he was the first American chief executive to visit Europe, or any foreign land, while in office. His was a mission of peace and personal diplomacy, a continuation of his crusade to make the world "safe for democracy." It was a journey widely heralded by the ordinary folk of Europe, who were much impressed by Wilson's idealism and his hopes for the future. Italians put his picture in the windows of their homes and many a peasant burned candles before it. Ray Stannard Baker related that university men in Poland used his name as a greeting, crying out "Wilson!" when they met and shook hands. Paris eagerly awaited his coming, and the city was decorated with banners bearing the words "Honor to Wilson the Just." There was a general, if undefined, feeling that the tall, sober American could heal all the earth's long-festering sores. With him he brought proposals for settlements, some of which were not even related to the Allied or Central powers, or even to the recent war.

It was Wilson's hope that a peace settlement could be made on the basis

The home front was mobilized by posters like this one exhorting people to plant war gardens and can their vegetables—and so "can" the German Kaiser, Wilhelm II, too.

of the Fourteen Points he had laid before Congress early in 1918. Principally they had called for freedom of the seas; the end of secret diplomacy and artificial trade barriers; arms reduction; a settlement of colonial claims; German evacuation of Russia, Belgium, and France; the redrawing of national boundaries and self-determination for all people. The 14th, and most widely discussed, point suggested a general association, or league, of nations to guarantee political freedom to all nations, large and small alike.

American liberals enthusiastically accepted the idealistic aims of the Fourteen Points and, as long as the war lasted, the Allied powers appeared to share their feelings. Once the peace talks opened in Paris on January 18, 1919, however, the victorious European nations began to make specific territorial or financial

The horror of war is reflected in the gaunt faces of the German prisoners (at the center) and the wounded American soldiers, who stream back from the front during the Meuse-Argonne fighting of 1918.

demands that did not always fit the pattern of Wilson's more general proposals. The very size of the gathering created great difficulties. The British delegation filled five hotels, and at one time the Americans, ranging from high diplomats to clerks, numbered 1,300. It soon became apparent that a few of the leaders would have to make most of the decisions if any solutions were to be reached.

Wilson led the United States delegation; Premier Clemenceau and Marshal Foch represented France; Prime Minister David Lloyd George headed the British group; and Premier Vittorio Orlando spoke for the Italians.

No Germans were present at the preliminary sessions, for the Allies had long since decided to deny the vanquished any voice in the drafting of the treaty. They intended neither to listen to arguments from the Germans nor to haggle with them.

From January to May, the representatives worked at various problems, assembling details, searching for solutions. Directing the work was the Supreme Council, made up of two delegates apiece from the United States, Great Britain, France, Italy, and Japan. When this group proved to be somewhat unwieldy, it was reduced from 10 to five delegates. Then

Japan, which had played a relatively small role in the war, was dropped. After complaining that Italy was not getting all she had been promised, Orlando went home. This left only the Big Three to do the treaty-making.

The treaty

As Wilson, Clemenceau, and Lloyd George fashioned the general outline of the treaty, it became increasingly clear that most of Wilson's idealistic plans would be disregarded. The European members of the group were fully aware that Wilson's great dream was a League of Nations, and although they were in general agree-

ment that an organization of this kind was necessary, they also saw in the President's obsession a chance to gain concessions for their own countries. France demanded maximum protection against future aggressions by Germany, and with British support, she asked for reparations that would cripple her former enemy economically for years to come. For their part, the British objected to reducing armaments, because it would mean reducing the size of their navy, then the greatest in the world. The Italians were much upset by Wilson's refusal to grant them territory promised in the secret Treaty of London four years earlier. The Belgians, too, were dissatisfied and threatened to boycott the sessions. At this point, the Japanese demanded Germany's former rights in the Chinese Shantung Peninsula, asserting that they had been promised to them. When Wilson yielded, he alienated the Chinese, who subsequently refused to sign the treaty. To cap it all, American-Irish groups said Wilson was not working hard enough for Irish independence and denounced him as a British puppet. On the other hand, Clemenceau thought he was pro-German, while the Italians accused him of favoring their rivals, the Yugoslavs. The President was also sharply attacked at home by Republican protectionists in the Senate for his desire to eliminate economic trade barriers.

After long and acrimonious arguments, in which Wilson often re-treated to ward off further attacks upon his cherished league, a treaty was drawn up. The signing took place at Versailles on June 28, 1919, the fifth anniversary of the assassination of the Austrian Archduke Francis Ferdinand. Germany was ordered to agree to a document that not only fixed guilt for the war upon her but directed her to pay its entire cost. Even Wilson the Just did not object to the terms. "I believe," he said in defense of his stand, "that a hard peace is a good thing for Germany herself, in order that she may know what an unjust war means."

Whether it was a good or a just treaty, it did not provide a lasting peace. It was sharply criticized by the liberals of the time, because too many of Wilson's Fourteen Points had been lost. To be sure, such doctrines as the self-determination of peoples appeared in the treaty, but even this laudable idea was badly distorted in the whittling-down and compromising. Although the treaty had limitations in its attempts to arrive at settlements, its greatest weakness lay in the economic penalties levied on the German nation. Had these strictures been less harsh, there would have been less reason for the discontent that paved the way for Adolf Hitler's rise a few years later. If the price demanded had not been so unrealistically high, the German people might have been willing to attempt to pay it. But the bill charged them totaled more than the value of the entire gold supply in the

The victorious war leaders met in Paris in 1919 for a settlement of the massive conflict—(left to right) Lloyd George, Orlando, Clemenceau, and Wilson.

world at that time. To make it worse, when Germany tried to pay off her debt by trading with such countries as the United States, high tariffs made it impossible. Thus it was not hard for rabble-rousers like Hitler to use the widespread hatred of the Versailles Treaty to win support.

Treaty wrecking in the Senate

During the months that Democrat Wilson labored at the Paris peace table, his Republican opponents in the Senate prepared their battle lines and awaited his return. They resented the fact that their party, which had gained control of the Senate in the 1918 elections, was practically ignored by the President, and they resolved to take their revenge when the treaty came up for ratification.

Had Wilson been less inflexible, he might have saved his League of Nations. During February, 1919, he made a short trip home from Paris to sign some bills and to consult with the Senate Foreign Relations Committee. Early the next month, 39 Senators and Senators-elect presented him with a statement to the effect that any discussion of the league should wait until a peace treaty was signed. The President flatly refused to consider the idea.

Led by Senators William Borah of Idaho and Henry Cabot Lodge of Massachusetts, a small group of "irreconcilables" determined to kill the league, even if they had to reject the entire treaty in the process. But Wilson's opponents needed time to organize their forces. First they insisted that all 264 pages of the document be read before the Senate. This took two weeks. Then came six more weeks of public hearings. During this period, the treaty opponents enlisted the aid of such wealthy men as Henry Clay Frick and Andrew Mellon, whose money financed a massive propaganda attack throughout the nation.

While speakers launched their attacks in public places, the treaty wreckers in the Senate, led by Lodge, went to work in earnest. By September, 1919, the Foreign Relations Committee reported that it had added 45 amendments and four reservations. When Congress voted them down, Lodge's committee came right back with additional reservations, the most important of which was a provision that the United States had no obligation to protect the territorial integrity or political independence of any other nation.

Meanwhile, the grave, introspective schoolmaster in the White House was not willing to stand by and watch his creation ripped to pieces. Tired and worn from his nerve-racking trials at the peace conference, he still somehow found the strength to fight back; it would prove the final battle of his life. His eloquent pleas before the Senate had been received coldly as "glittering generalities" and "soap bubbles of oratory." Now he had no choice but to carry his crusade to the ultimate source of power—the voters.

In the fall of 1919, he undertook a journey that carried him across the nation—8,000 miles in 22 days—during which he delivered 37 long addresses. But on September 25, at Pueblo, Colorado, exhaustion overcame him, and in a state of near collapse he returned quickly to Washington. A week later, he was stricken with a near-fatal paralytic stroke.

During November, as Wilson lay ill, the Senators concluded their vivisection of the treaty. The irreconcilables managed to attach 15 reservations and so burdened it that there was no possibility of the necessary two-thirds vote for ratification. In an effort to put an official end to America's participation in the war, Congress in May, 1920, adopted a joint resolution repealing the declaration of war against the Central Powers. Still pressing for acceptance of his version of the treaty, Wilson vetoed it. There the matter stood until Warren G. Harding was inaugurated. In July, 1921, he signed the resolution, and in this vacillating way America formally ended its part in the "great crusade."

U.S. AIR FORCE

THE WAR IN THE AIR

When World War I began in 1914, France had a relatively large air force—260 planes—and 191 trained pilots. Germany had a mere 46 planes, England only 29. None of these were armed, and it was assumed that they would be used solely for observation. Soon, however, the rival pilots took to firing pistols and rifles at one another as they passed in the air. Then the Frenchman Roland Garros put metal deflectors on his propeller so he could use a forward-firing machine gun without splintering the propeller. Next, a Dutchman named Anthony Fokker, who was working for Germany, invented a synchronizing gear that permitted a machine gun to fire only when the propeller was not in the way, and a truly efficient system of making war in the air had been found. Planes could now strafe enemy troops and shoot down enemy aircraft to prevent observation. There were some primitive attempts at bombing, but in the early days it was generally the single-seater pursuit ship against another single-seater or an observation plane, as above: French ace Georges Guynemer in his Spad has just shot down a German two-seater carrying pilot and observer.

1105

Oswald Boelcke (above, left) used Fokker's synchronizing gear and became Germany's first ace with 40 kills before he crashed in October, 1916. The Fokker he is flying was the finest fighter of 1915—capable of the then-amazing 93 miles per hour.

A wounded flyer (below) hangs over the rim of his cockpit while his mate pilots the plane home. This craft was called a "pusher" because the propeller was in the rear. The design with the engine behind the pilot had a brief popularity during 1914–15.

THE KNIGHTS OF THE SKY

Baron Manfred von Richthofen, the Red Knight of Germany, had 80 victories, the largest score made by any pilot on either side during the war, before Canadian Captain Roy Brown got on the tail of the baron's Fokker triplane and, perhaps assisted by Australian ground-fire (above, right), shot him down on April 21, 1918, with a bullet in the chest.

OVERLEAF: A pilot of the Lafayette Escadrille begins a strafing run. The squadron was formed in April, 1916, and it included seven young Americans who had volunteered with the French. Eventually, 38 Americans flew with the famous Indian-head unit.

U.S. AIR FORCE

FAMOUS AIRPLANES: 1914–1918

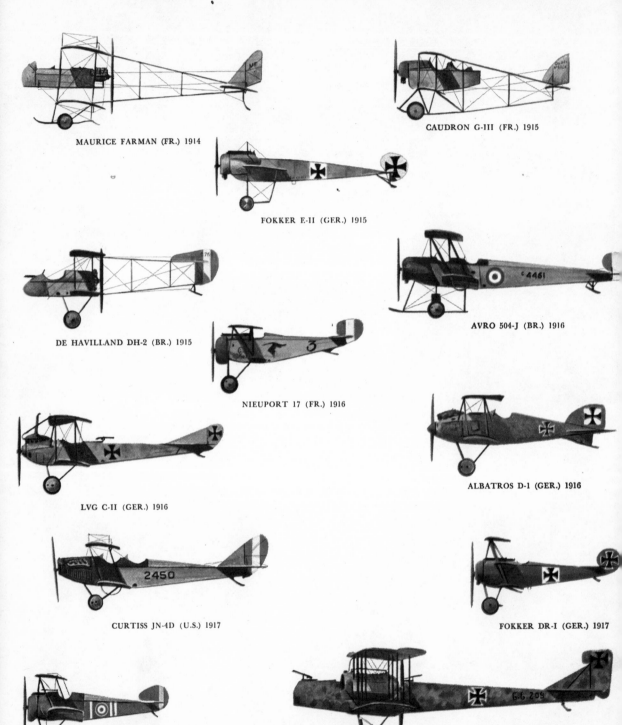

MAURICE FARMAN (FR.) 1914

CAUDRON G-III (FR.) 1915

FOKKER E-II (GER.) 1915

DE HAVILLAND DH-2 (BR.) 1915

AVRO 504-J (BR.) 1916

NIEUPORT 17 (FR.) 1916

LVG C-II (GER.) 1916

ALBATROS D-1 (GER.) 1916

CURTISS JN-4D (U.S.) 1917

FOKKER DR-I (GER.) 1917

SOPWITH CAMEL (BR.) 1917

GOTHA G-V BOMBER (GER.) 1917

BRISTOL F-2B (BR.) 1917

SPAD 13 (FR.) 1917

BREGUET 14 (FR.) 1917

SE-5 (BR.) 1917

FOKKER D-VII (GER.) 1918

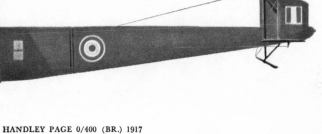

HANDLEY PAGE 0/400 (BR.) 1917

JUNKERS D-I (GER.) 1918

AMERICAN DH-4 (BR.-U.S.) 1918

LOENING M-8 (U.S.) 1918

NAVY-CURTISS F-5L (U.S.) 1918

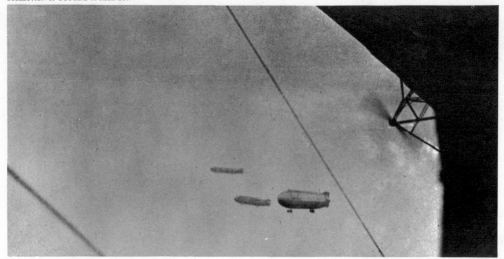

THE WAR IN THE AIR

TERROR RAIDS
ON LONDON

In January, 1915, the German Naval Airship Division began to bomb London by zeppelin, and the British retaliated with barrage balloons (below). Lieutenant Reginald Warneford won the Victoria Cross by dropping six 20-pound bombs on an enemy craft (right) and setting her afire.

"BOMBS AWAY"

When the zeppelins failed, the Germans bombed England with Gotha bombers (above). Although they carried 1,500 pounds of bombs, they inflicted only slight damage in 52 raids.

The Allies tried bombing and spotting, with planes like the French Caudron (above), and night bombing (below) when antiaircraft losses made day raids too expensive. Not until 1918 did British General Hugh Trenchard receive permission for true strategic bombing—raids on German cities and factories.

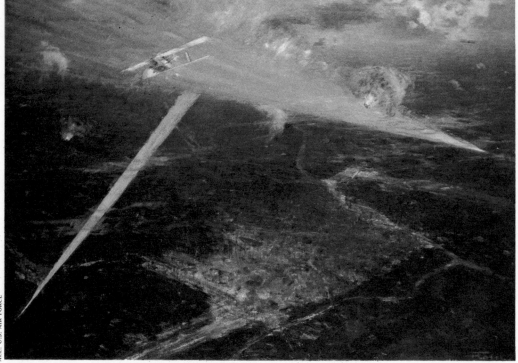

BOELCKE

FONCK

NUNGESSER

BISHOP

MANNOCK

These were some of the leading pilots. From the top, left: Oswald Boelcke, German ace and teacher of aces; Rene Fonck, top French ace with 75 kills. Frenchman Charles Nungesser later died trying to fly the Atlantic. Canadian ace Billy Bishop shot down 72 planes; Edward "Mick" Mannock led the English with 73 victories. The American Frank Luke was an expert at knocking down German observation balloons. Manfred von Richthofen is shown with members of his Flying Circus. Eddie Rickenbacker, top American ace, made 26 kills. He led the Hat in the Ring squadron.

RICHTHOFEN (top, center)

LUKE

RICKENBACKER

CHAPTER 38

THE BUSINESSMAN'S GOVERNMENT

Johnny came marching home from the trenches to a country tired of sacrifice and idealism. Amid the confusion of returning to a peacetime economy and way of life, there grew a feeling of disillusion—a conviction that the expenditure of American blood and treasure on the battlefields of Europe had been for nothing. As the desire to make the world "safe for democracy" gave way to a quest for individual prosperity and security, people lost interest in foreign affairs. They began to feel nostalgic for the good old prewar days. President Warren G. Harding expressed it with the words "return to normalcy."

Nothing, in fact, demonstrated this longing for "normalcy" more than the election of the genial and innocuous Senator from Ohio. During 1920, as Americans made ready to choose a successor to the professor-President, Wilson, there was a desire, perhaps unconscious, to forget the crusades of the past eight years. The political tide

The Allies Day parade on New York's Fifth Avenue, painted by Childe Hassam, symbolizes Allied unity when America entered World War I—a unity ending with the war.

was running Republican—a trend that had become apparent two years earlier after the G.O.P.'s victories in the 1918 Congressional elections.

By the time the Republican convention met at Chicago in June, party members were buoyantly confident. Flushed with their recent triumph over Wilson and the League of Nations, the conservatives took charge.

As it was probable that the Republican Party's nominee would be the next President, droves of candidates made their availability known. Perhaps the only person who seemed sure of the result was Henry M. Daugherty, a small-town Ohio lawyer. A man with considerable influence in the party in his home state, he predicted as early as February that the convention would arrive at a deadlock. Then, about two o'clock in the morning, Daugherty continued, "some 15 men, bleary-eyed with loss of sleep and perspiring profusely with the excessive heat, will sit down at a big table. I will be with them and will present the name of Senator Harding· to them, and before we get through, they will put him over." Harding was indeed "put over" in just that way. Governor

President Harding poses with his original cabinet—(seated, left to right) John W. Weeks, Andrew W. Mellon, Charles Evans Hughes, Harding, Vice-President Calvin Coolidge, Edwin Denby; (standing) Albert B. Fall, Will H. Hays, Henry M. Daugherty, Henry C. Wallace, Herbert Hoover, and J. J. Davis.

Calvin Coolidge of Massachusetts, whose one claim to national recognition had been his suppression of the Boston police strike in 1919, was nominated for the Vice-Presidency.

The unfavorable press reaction to the nomination gave the Democrats hope. One New York paper characterized Harding as "a very respectable Ohio politician of the second class" and his Senate record as "faint and colorless." And the Republicans produced a platform to match their candidate. The question of a League of Nations was handled so that it offended no one. Businessmen were wooed by promises to return the railroads and the merchant marine to private ownership and to give greater protection to manufacturers through tariff increases. The tendency of federal centralization, marked in the last years of the Wilson administration, was condemned.

The Democrats tried to capitalize upon Harding's weaknesses and upon Wilson's record. They nominated Governor James Cox of Ohio for President and Assistant Secretary of the Navy Franklin D. Roosevelt to run with him. The party promised to work for ratification of the peace treaty (although it did not oppose qualifying reservations), and to carry on the principles of Wilson's New Freedom. But neither the candidates nor their platforms had much appeal for the voters. Harding sat at home in Marion, Ohio, and let the public's desire for a change carry him to victory. On November 2, his 55th birthday, he was elected in a landslide, with 16,152,200 votes to 9,147,353 for Cox.

Harding's cabinet appointees were a measure of the lackluster quality of the man. In probably his best appointment, he made Charles Evans Hughes Secretary of State, mainly because, as he said, Hughes had been "approximately" elected President in 1916. Andrew Mellon, the Pittsburgh millionaire, headed the Treasury Department; Albert B. Fall of New Mexico became Secretary of the Interior; and as a reward for his efforts at the Republican convention, Harry Daugherty was made Attorney General. Except for Hughes, only the appointment of Henry C. Wallace as Secre-

tary of Agriculture and Herbert Hoover as Secretary of Commerce added distinction to Harding's cabinet. A number of lesser government offices went to members of the "Ohio gang," as Harding's intimates were known.

Harding's normalcy

When Harding called for a return to normalcy, it was understood that he wanted to go back to the "good old days," but exactly how far back he did not say. Politically, he seemed to have returned his party—and the

The sidelined Democratic Party exults over the unsavory oil scandals in the administration of the Republican Harding.

Its attitude different from that in the previous cartoon, the Democratic Party joins the Republican Party in wishing the Senate would find a distraction.

nation—to the era of McKinley. High tariffs and hands off big business were the rule; the progressive politics of Roosevelt and Wilson were shunned like a bad memory. As for morals, Harding's administration, with its blight of fraud and corruption, seemed a throwback to General Grant's.

In the beginning, the nation suspected none of this. Harding was personally popular, and his friendly attitude toward business satisfied the conservative temper of the times. In at least one instance, the Washington Conference for the Limitation of Armament, which produced a treaty limiting the naval armaments of the major powers, the administration could boast a significant, if regrettably short-lived, accomplishment. But from behind the placid facade, one scandal after another erupted into the open. The most spectacular was the Teapot Dome affair, in which Secretary of the Interior Albert B. Fall and Secretary of the Navy Edwin Denby were accused of giving oilmen Edward Doheny and Harry Sinclair access to valuable oil reserves set aside for the navy. In 1922, Doheny leased the Elk Hills reserve in California and Sinclair leased the Teapot Dome reserve in Wyoming. In return, the federal government received only some oil-storage tanks in Hawaii. A Senate investigation showed that Doheny had loaned $100,000 to Fall in 1921 without interest or collateral, and that after Fall had resigned from the cabinet in 1923, Sinclair had "loaned" him $250,000. Fall was convicted of bribery and sentenced to serve one year in prison and to pay a $100,000 fine. The Supreme Court declared the oil leases invalid in 1927.

Harding himself was personally honest, but that was more than could be said for some of his friends. The Veterans Bureau scandal was one example of the President's naive trust in people. On a visit to Hawaii he met and was impressed by one Charles R. Forbes, a jovial go-getter whose chief distinction was his courageous war record—although, oddly enough, it turned out that he had once been an army deserter. In 1921, Harding appointed his newfound friend custodian of veterans' affairs. During the two years Forbes held the office, $200,000,000 went astray. Contracts for hospital construction were let without regard to low bidders, and "surplus" goods were sold at unbelievably low prices, after which similar items were bought at the going market rate. In 1926, Forbes was sentenced to the federal penitentiary for two years and fined $10,000.

Another Harding appointee, Alien Property Custodian Thomas W. Miller, and a member of the Ohio gang named Jesse Smith made $100,000 in a transaction involving the return of the American Metal Company to its former German owners. Part of the money went to Attorney General Harry Daugherty. Miller went to prison for fraud; Smith committed suicide. When Daugherty refused to testify before a Senate investigating committee, Harding's successor, Coolidge, dismissed him.

Most of the scandals broke after Harding's death on August 2, 1923, midway through his term. Montana's two Senators, Thomas J. Walsh and Burton K. Wheeler, exposed the Teapot Dome giveaway and investigated irregularities in the Justice Department. Harding himself perhaps best explained his difficulties when he told journalist William Allen White, "I have no trouble with my enemies. . . . But my damned friends—they're the ones that keep me walking the floor nights!"

Calvin the Cool

When Calvin Coolidge succeeded Harding, America had a President who was as different from his predecessor as any man could be. The quiet New Englander had been almost unnoticed as Vice-President. Summarizing his meager duties, William Allen White wrote, "So Coolidge, silently dining and meekly clowning his quiet way through official Washington society by night and watching the Senate by day with no responsibilities, no anxieties, except to send a part of his pay check every month back to his Northampton bank to watch the $25,000 grow and grow—symbolizing the doctrine, work and save—he was, as it were, politically embalmed."

As President, Coolidge was in many ways a stranger to the Roaring Twen-

ties. It had been many years since Americans had seen a farm boy enter the White House, and now, in this new age of mechanization and urbanization, Coolidge seemed somehow a relic of the vanished past. But it did not take the businessman long to discover that in certain respects the new President was in tune with the times: His conservatism, his thorough advocacy of *laissez faire*, and his admiration of the masters of capital soon made him a favorite of the business community.

When the Republicans met at Cleveland in 1924, the convention was well organized for Coolidge and he was easily nominated. The Democratic candidate, John W. Davis, was a wealthy corporation lawyer. That year the Progressive Party made its final bid for the Presidency, nominating Robert LaFollette of Wisconsin and Burton K. Wheeler. LaFollette did get his own state's 13 electoral votes, but the nation was not seriously tempted to elect a reform candidate at a time of unbounded prosperity. In spite of the scandals of the Harding administration, voters followed the injunction of Republican Party leaders to "Keep cool with Coolidge" and returned the prim, silent "Cal" to office by a majority of 382 to 136 electoral votes.

Late in the summer of 1927, Calvin Coolidge went fishing in the Black Hills of South Dakota. Reporters had come along on the off-chance that "Silent Cal" might say something of

In May, 1932, the magazine Vanity Fair *was still spoofing Coolidge's well-known taciturnity by pairing him with Greta Garbo in its series of "impossible interviews."*

interest. He did. One day he crisply announced, "I do not choose to run for President in 1928." That was all.

This surprising decision produced the usual crop of favorite sons and other prospective candidates, but Herbert Hoover, well known to Americans for his brilliant record in war relief and his capable performance as a cabinet member under both Hard-

1125

ing and Coolidge, was easily the strongest. When the Republicans convened at Kansas City in June, 1928, the Secretary of Commerce was duly nominated.

Meanwhile, the Democrats passed up popular Governor Albert C. Ritchie of Maryland, and Montana's Senator Thomas J. Walsh of Teapot Dome fame, in favor of New York's flamboyant Governor Alfred E. Smith. A product of the slums of Manhattan's Lower East Side, the "Happy Warrior" (as Franklin D. Roosevelt called him), was chosen on the first ballot. But once again Democratic prospects were poor, for Smith, who was both

The exuberance of Al Smith, the Irishman from the slums of New York who ran for President, is caught in this caricature.

wet and a Catholic, faced an uphill fight in a nation that was both dry and predominantly Protestant.

"Sweep the country with Hoover"

In the contest that followed, issues were largely evaded. A vicious whispering campaign made it appear that Smith's bad grammar and the threat of Papal interference at the White House were equally great dangers to the nation's future. Virtually overlooked as an issue was the facade of paper prosperity behind which there were urgent problems that demanded solution (ominously enough, just two days before Hoover was nominated, the stock market suffered a brief and near-disastrous crash). Hoover and his running mate, Senator Charles Curtis, said little about such matters, but their silence seemed to have its reward: They won by 444 to 87 electoral votes—the third Republican landslide in a row. As the Democrats discovered to their chagrin, prosperity was unbeatable at the polls.

When Hoover took office in March, 1929, the country welcomed him as the ideal successor to Coolidge. He objected to any government interference in business affairs on the ground that it was detrimental not only to economic life but to liberty itself. As he said during the campaign, "Economic freedom cannot be sacrificed if political freedom is to be preserved." In 1929, these were the words that perfectly matched the mood of the nation. Few could foresee that America was on the verge of the worst depression in its history.

In retrospect, the roaring aspect of the Roaring Twenties seems like a gaudy false front for a structure that was beginning to show signs of an alarming deterioration from within. Behind the bright exterior, serious stresses and strains could be detected, and although a variety of remedies were tried, most would prove tragically shortsighted.

For example, the tariff issue had not lost any of its perplexities, and its ramifications went much farther than simply offering protection to American farms and factories. At a time when isolationism and a desire for economic self-sufficiency prevailed, high-tariff proponents had little difficulty in persuading Congress to pass the Fordney-McCumber Tariff of 1922, which contained the highest rates in the nation's history. The result was disastrous. International trade, which had been growing steadily since the war's end, was checked, and other nations adopted retaliatory tariffs, causing American exports to diminish even more. Even more prohibitive was the Smoot-Hawley Tariff of 1930. At Hoover's suggestion, tariff makers were set to work in an attempt to protect the American farmer from foreign competition. Before they were through, a thousand tariff increases were suggested, all but 75 of which were for industry, not agriculture. Within two years, 25 countries had retaliated, raising their own tariffs.

On Inauguration Day, 1929, Coolidge, looking more solemn than usual, stands next to President-elect Herbert Hoover.

Instead of gaining the needed trade, Americans watched their exports continue to fall off. As far as commerce was concerned, this act of "splendid isolation" merely deepened the depression then under way.

Transportation was another economic problem of the '20s. America's merchant marine, for example, found itself in increasingly serious difficulties. During the war, it had been controlled by the government, but when peace came, there was a great demand to return it to private hands. As a result of the Merchant Marine Act of

1920, ships were sold to individuals and to shipping companies on most reasonable terms. Moreover, preferential rates were given to goods and persons carried to the United States from foreign countries in American ships. And subsidies of from $30,-000,000 to $50,000,000 a year were paid to companies whose income was not great enough to meet their cost of operation. The act even went so far as to restrict trade with American colonial possessions to American ships —a mercantilist policy that seemed almost a throwback to the 18th century. Yet for all these inducements, the business done by American shipping lines declined steadily during the decade. High wages, high construction costs, and high operating expenses were blamed for the nation's inability to compete with foreign shipping companies. The postwar years also saw a changed policy toward the railroads. Wilson had set the tone in his annual message to Congress in December, 1918, when he criticized a course of "restraint without development."

The Transportation Act of 1920 returned the roads to private ownership, and at the same time laid down rules for a new kind of control. Although the Interstate Commerce Commission was empowered to govern rates, the railroads were assured a return on their investment of at least 5 1/2%. A "recapture clause" provided that one-half of all earnings above 6% should be turned over to the government and put in a revolving fund for the benefit of the weaker roads. Instead of "trust busting," the act took a long step toward consolidation under government sponsorship—a step that fell just short of nationalization.

A much newer industry, which presented problems of its own, was electric power. By 1920, the majority of American homes had electricity, and with the abundance of new electrical appliances on the market, the industry mushroomed. That year a Federal Power Commission came into existence. Although it was authorized to issue licenses for the construction and operation of facilities for the development of electric power, experience showed that it had little ability to control rates or services. Nor was it able to regulate the growth and spread of huge power monopolies. As local companies merged into larger organizations, they in turn became components of huge holding companies. By 1920, about 12 of these systems controlled more than 75% of the power generated in the nation. One man, Samuel Insull of Chicago, pyramided his holding and investment companies until he had interests in nearly 4,800 communities in 30 different states. Insull was chairman of the board of 65 different companies and the president of 11 others. But as time went on, he overextended himself. His stocks were heavily watered, and when the crash came in 1929, the dam burst. His empire gone, Insull fled the country; he died leaving $1,000 in cash and debts of $14,000,000. It

The merchant ships that were built by the government during the war, in ship-yards like this one painted by Jonas Lie, were afterward sold to private companies.

was disasters of that kind that would later help to convince the public that greater federal control and even federally built and operated power projects were in its best interests.

The business of farming

By the 1920s the American farmer had become something of a businessman himself. The age-old figure of the honest plowman following the endless single furrow had given way to that of an agricultural technician operating expensive gasoline-driven machinery; the day of the small farmer was rapidly passing. Now powerful tractors pulled multiple plows in the springtime and complicated, costly wheat combines in the fall.

When the decade began, the prospects for American agriculture had seemed bright. Wartime prices had been high—artificially high. But in the next few years, American markets in Europe dwindled as that battered continent recovered from the effects of the war and was once more able to feed its own population. To complicate matters, farms had to face an increasingly fierce competition in the export of such basic commodities as grain from countries like Russia, Canada, Australia, and Argentina. The price of agricultural goods, sold on a world market, sank steadily. In an attempt to counter the ill effects of this decline, American farmers tried to cut their losses by growing bigger crops. But prices merely continued to plummet, and as the costs of the machinery necessary for large-scale operations multiplied, the farmer found himself ever more deeply in debt.

Legislative attempts to help agriculture were older than the national government itself. From the time of the Ordinance of 1785, under the Articles of Confederation, lawmakers had tried to aid Americans who lived off the soil. In 1921, Congress tried once more, this time raising the tariff duties on foreign agricultural products. As the United States exported more foodstuffs than it imported, the maneuver accomplished little or nothing. The farm bloc in Congress also pushed through the Packers and Stockyards Act (1921) in an attempt to break up packing-company monopolies that were accused of taking too large a profit. The Grain Futures Trading Act was similarly designed to put a stop to monopolies and price manipulations in the grain market. The Capper-Volstead Cooperative Marketing Act (1922) attempted to protect small farmers who had grouped together in cooperatives by exempting them from prosecution under the Sherman Antitrust Act.

More tangible help came in the form of loans. In 1921, Congress enlarged the powers of the War Finance Corporation by allowing it to extend aid to farmers. The Federal Intermediate Credit Act of 1923 set up 12 regional banks and provided each institution with $5,000,000. By 1930, farmers had borrowed a total of $3,000,000,000 from the various sources available to them.

Such efforts were helpful, but they were essentially no more than stopgap measures. During the whole decade of the '20s, the one attempt to get to the root of the farm problem was the McNary-Haugen Farm Relief Bill. It provided for a federal farm board to fix the local price of grain and buy the surplus. This would either be stored until the price rose or sold abroad at the going world-market price. To compensate for the loss if the federal farm board had to sell outside the country, the bill proposed that the government levy an "equalization fee" against grain sold on the domestic market. Twice the act passed Congress and twice Coolidge vetoed it, for he believed it included a price-fixing principal and also benefited special groups and was therefore unconstitutional.

More successful was the Agricultural Marketing Bill, passed in 1929 and signed by Hoover. It established an eight-member Federal Farm Board, headed by the Secretary of Agriculture, to encourage the development of agricultural cooperatives and to make loans to them. The board tried to buy up surplus wheat and managed, in 1931, to raise the price 20¢ to 30¢ above the going rate on the world market. It did the same with cotton. But when surpluses became too great to buy up, the program collapsed, and agricultural prices fell to new lows. Hoover discovered, as would his successors, that merely buying surpluses would not and could not solve the problem of overproduction.

The plight of the worker

The farmer was not the only one who stood back and enviously watched the businessman enjoy the biggest boom in the nation's history, for the industrial worker, too, did not always share in the general prosperity. Many people believed that labor had significantly bettered its lot during the war, but its gains were largely superficial. It is true that during 1914–18 the major union organization—the American Federation of Labor—had doubled its strength. In 1920, it stood at the peak of its power, with 4,000,000 members. Within a decade, however, membership had fallen by over 1,000,000. One reason was the apathy of the labor movement itself; another was the prevailing conservatism of the period, which regarded organized labor as a threat to continued prosperity.

Organized labor did little to combat the adverse trend. When Samuel Gompers died in 1924 and William Green took over the A.F.L., the organization seemed to become a dig-

By 1920, the days of the small farmer were numbered, and powerful tractors like the one above were making possible the development of large farm operations.

Millworker John Kane painted Turtle Creek Valley's steelworks in Pennsylvania in 1922, when a recession had set in and organized labor was losing ground.

nified, conservative, and even timid satellite of big business, retaining few of its old crusading instincts. Corporations followed a policy of "killing with kindness" any segments of labor that threatened to be aggressive. Workers were encouraged, through the distribution of various benefits, to join company-sponsored unions. By mid-decade there were more than 400 of these organizations, with their total membership half that of those affiliated with the A.F.L. But the leadership of the A.F.L. seemed uninclined to fight back. It quietly accepted the rise of the company unions, making no real attempt to remain independ-

ent of what has been called welfare capitalism.

Nor was the businessman's government taking any chances on a labor resurgence. The hostility of the courts rivaled that of the 1890s. In *Hammer vs. Dagenhart* (1918) and *Bailey vs. Drexel Furniture Company* (1922), the Supreme Court quashed the efforts of Congress to end child labor. Also, there was a growing use of the injunction in labor disputes. The Supreme Court struck hard at labor in *Coppage vs. Kansas* (1915) when it upheld the yellow-dog contract—one that forbids employees to join a union. In *Adkins vs. Children's Hospital*

When Thomas Hart Benton painted his oil-rich Boom Town *in 1928, the Harding administration's oil scandals were still before the public and the courts.*

(1923) the court ruled, in effect, that minimum wage laws were unconstitutional. Labor still had the right to boycott, strike, and picket despite these decisions, but the laws were made so restrictive that even these traditional weapons were badly weakened.

The isolationist impulse

A part of the prevailing political conservatism of the '20s was isolationism. There seemed to be a desire to retreat within America's ramparts and let the rest of the world take care of its own problems. During the early part of Harding's administration, communications from the League of Nations were not even answered, and the government refused, in reality, to recognize its existence. Throughout the '20s and '30s, the United States declined membership in the World Court, even though every President from Harding to Franklin D. Roosevelt recommended participation. Each attempt to join was blocked by the Senate, either by outright rejection or by the inclusion of reservations that member nations would not accept.

The main exception to this lonewolf policy was the Washington Conference in 1921. America emerged from the war as the world's leading

1133

economic power; if its wartime program of armament had been continued, she would have become the dominant military and naval power as well.

In August, 1921, Secretary of State Charles Evans Hughes invited all major powers except Russia to a conference on the limitation of armaments. There was a willing response; Great Britain in particular had little desire to maintain a huge military establishment that had to be financed by exorbitant taxes. The purpose of the conference was twofold: One was to consider naval disarmament, and the other was to discuss ways of easing tensions in the Pacific and the Far East, where the Western nations felt their colonial interests were being threatened by the rapid and increasingly militant expansion of the Japanese Empire. Representatives from the United States, Great Britain, France, Italy, and Japan, as well as those from such minor powers as China, Belgium, the Netherlands, and Portugal attended. Meeting at Washington for the first time on November 12, the diplomats negotiated until February 6, 1922. Their work is most often remembered for the naval disarmament treaty, one of nine it produced. In this treaty, the United States, Great Britain, and Japan agreed to a limitation of the number of battleships in their fleets. The first two were to be allowed 500,000 tons each, Japan was to have 300,000 tons —or a ratio of 5-5-3. To their disappointment, France and Italy were obliged to settle for 175,000 tons each.

Two of the other treaties dealt with the Far Eastern problem. In one involving the United States, Great Britain, France, and Japan, the signers agreed to respect the rights of one another in the Pacific and to refer all major disputes to arbitration. A nine-power treaty, signed by the "Big Five" as well as Holland, Portugal, China, and Belgium, pledged the territorial integrity of China and reaffirmed the open-door principle.

Later, in 1927, President Coolidge called for the five great powers to meet at Geneva to consider limitations on ships not covered by the naval disarmament treaty. France and Italy refused to attend, and the United States, Britain, and Japan could not agree upon a formula. The failure put a strain on Anglo-American relations and foreshadowed Japan's later unwillingness to abide by the earlier agreement.

A final gesture toward permanent world peace was the Kellogg-Briand Pact of 1928, put forward by the United States and France. This idealistic document, which attempted to "outlaw" war "as an instrument of national policy," was approved by 15 nations (62 eventually signed it). Although widely popular, it was to prove ineffectual; as Senator David A. Reed of Missouri said, it was little more than an "international kiss." Events of the next decade would bear tragic witness that war could not be abolished by the flourish of a pen.

NEW YORK PUBLIC LIBRARY

AMERICA AS ADVERTISED

From World War I through the '20s, advertising reflected the opulence and the taboos of the times. The Arrow collar (above) spread its full-dress wings. The better automobiles abandoned dependability as their chief sales theme and became status symbols. Bathroom fixtures were not yet seen in full, but peeked at through curtains of Oriental richness. The home heater was for the living room, just as the pipe organ was. Girls did not smoke in advertisements—only encouraged their men to do so. Jell-O was pictured, by Maxfield Parrish, as fit for king and queen. Cosmetics and women's shoes and hosiery were presented by *femmes fatales,* but corsets, underwear, and swimming suits were offered with no help from alluring female figures. As for the men's-wear models, Mother Nature would not have recognized them. These old advertisements speak for themselves, without captions.

PIERCE-ARROW

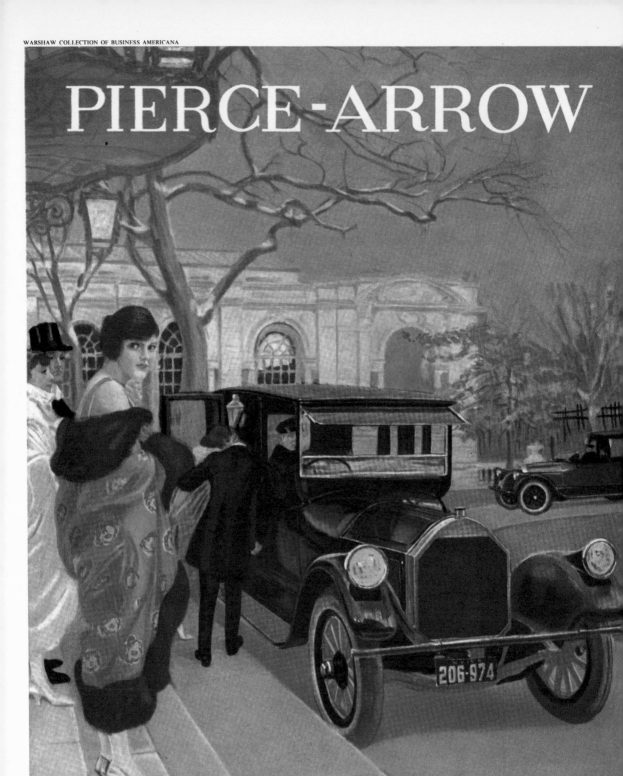

*N*O *words* do justice to the fine feeling that the new
PIERCE-ARROW gives—the fine feeling of power am-
ple and unfailing, so perfectly applied that the car increases
its service and comfort with nothing to detract from them.

THE PIERCE ARROW MOTOR CAR COMPANY · BUFFALO, NEW YO

CHRYSLER MOTORS PRODUCT

Chrysler Imperial Convertible Coupe (wire wheels extra), $1995

IMPERIAL

THE new Chrysler Imperial is a car intended essentially for the connoisseurs among motorists—that exclusive circle whose discrimination is satisfied with nothing short of the best in Chrysler power, smoothness, fineness and beauty. ¶ The distinguished characteristics of the Chrysler Imperial reveal the latest and utmost ingenuity of Chrysler styling, engineering and craftsmanship. ¶ Every motorist who appreciates a car of true custom quality will find in the new Imperial a type of beauty and behavior unlike and beyond anything heretofore known in the field of the very finest.

Roadster $1675; Sedan (5-passenger), $1795; Town Sedan, $1795; Standard Coupe, $1995; Convertible Coupe, $1995; Phaeton (7-passenger), $1995; Sedan (7-passenger), $2095; Sedan Limousine, $2475; Custom-built Phaeton (4-passenger), $3855. All prices f. o. b. factory.

PHAETON
Four-Passenger

COLE
Eight Ninety

It has been the privilege of the producers of the Cole to incorporate in its building those features that mark it as

truly

A FINER CAR

COLE MOTOR CAR COMPANY
INDIANAPOLIS, U. S. A.

There's a Touch of Tomorrow in All Cole Cars Today

Seven Passenger Sedan

The distinguished Lincoln clientele includes many who prefer the popular Sedan body type so admirably adapted to family use. They are content with no less than Lincoln well-balanced excellence, luxurious appointments, body beauty and obedient, effortless performance. The magnificent Seven-Passenger Sedan is designed for these Lincoln patrons.

LINCOLN MOTOR COMPANY
Division of Ford Motor Company

A Charming Something with lithe and youthful lines— a thoroughbred descendant of a roving race —inspired with the verve of modern youth —and dressed up like nobody's business —in short ready to go somewhere —and going. That's the new Jordan Playboy.

"Standard"
PLUMBING FIXTURES

Standard Sanitary Mfg. Co.
Pittsburgh

The Magic Rug of the Twentieth Century

Magic! It's cleaned with a few whisks of a dry mop. *Magic!* It's made absolutely waterproof to insure long wear.
Magic! It's made on a felt base with an enamel-like surface in a score of patterns and colors. *Magic!* It's sold at retail in sizes and prices from $9 to $18 by scores of enormous production.

If every woman knew what every present owner knows, every home would have a Bird's Neponset Rug.
If any salesman says "It's Bird's" that's really all you need to know. Look for the patented red wax back.

NEW YORK ... CHICAGO ... DALLAS
PHILADELPHIA ... DURAND ... DENVER
ATLANTA ... ST. PAUL ... SEATTLE
SAN FRANCISCO ... LOS ANGELES

BIRD & SON, Inc.
Established 1795
Products in Felt-Base Floor Coverings
EAST WALPOLE, MASS.

Also makes: Bird's Twin Shingle, Bird's Paroid Roofing, Bird's Design, Roofing, Bird's Black Building Paper and Bird's Wall Board

Bird's Rugs
BIRD NEPONSET PRODUCTS

DEFY WATER AND WEAR

THE ESTEY RESIDENCE PIPE ORGAN

ONE THRILLS at the very idea of a pipe organ in the home. It is such a majestic instrument. It adds so much to the dignity, the unusualness of even the most complete and modern house. Its music is so satisfying. It appeals to all.

And a pipe organ is so easily attainable. We have solved all the problems. We are able to build an organ to fit any house, and at almost any price. The Estey Residence Organ can be played auto-matically by The Estey Organist, so that skill and training are unnecessary. But this does not interfere with its being a perfect instrument for the human player.

THE ESTEY ORGAN COMPANY, *Brattleboro, Vermont*

Studios in New York, 11 West 49th Street
CHICAGO, Lyon & Healy
PHILADELPHIA, 1701 Walnut Street
BOSTON, 120 Boylston Street
LOS ANGELES, 653 South Hill Street

A Welcome Addition to Any Home

LIKE the new arrival, ARCOLA is a most welcome and important addition, changing the house into a home, to benefit and gladden the entire family! In the days of creeping childhood and growing youth, there is greatest need to guard with reliable, protecting ARCOLA warmth, all floors, nooks and corners. Ideal ARCOLA Hot Water Heating will make the whole house a healthful playground—and a delightful relaxing place, as well, for grown-ups and the elderly.

ARCOLA keeps the rooms at 72°, all through—or at any other degree you set—regardless of weather changes. The Automatic Controler watches the fire, saving enough fuel in five years to repay cost of the ARCOLA. For the rest of your life you have a big interest-earning investment—the cleanliest, health-giving warmth for baby and all! Examine all the ARCOLA features at any heating and plumbing store. Note its handsome porcelain-enameled jacket. Burns ANY fuel. New low price due to great volume of sales.

ARCOLA
(T. M. Reg. U. S. Pat. Off.)
Hot Water Radiator Heat

Gives you the comfort you have always wanted! Enjoy an ARCOLA at once, and pay in ten months! If you have a small home, bungalow, single flat, store, shop, office, etc., write us, Dept. 1, 1807 Elmwood Ave., Buffalo, for (free) book on ARCOLA—full of valuable heating information. Make this fine addition to your home today!

AMERICAN RADIATOR COMPANY

Showrooms and sales offices: New York, Boston, Providence, Philadelphia, Baltimore, Washington, Buffalo, Pittsburgh, Cleveland, Detroit, Cincinnati, Atlanta, Chicago, Milwaukee, Indianapolis, St. Louis, St. Paul, Omaha, Kansas City, Denver, San Francisco, Los Angeles, Seattle
Toronto, London, Paris, Milan, Brussels, Berlin

Makers of IDEAL BOILERS

For larger buildings: Type "A" Machine, Arco, Water Tube, Soft Coal Smokeless; factory heating boilers and other heating, ventilating and cooling products

January 1926 Good Housekeeping

1139

Flowers of the Orient

AN added charm of Florient Talc is the color of the powder. This is most unusual and distinctive—just off the white. The rare Oriental fragrance and delicate fineness of the powder itself also explain the popularity of Colgate's Florient—the new superfine Talc.

Florient, you will remember, gained first place in an International Perfume Contest. As the pure delight of its fragrance won favor—so will the grace and beauty of the new box in which Florient Talc comes to you.

An attractive miniature box of Florient Talc will be sent upon request if you mention *Vogue*.

COLGATE & CO.   *Est. 1806*   **New York**

The exquisite fragrance of Florient is now embodied also in Extract Toilet Water, in Face Powder, and in Soap.

LILY OF FRANCE CORSET

THE LILY OF FRANCE IS A BEAUTIFUL
CORSET WORN BY BEAUTIFUL WOMEN
TO MAKE THEM MORE BEAUTIFUL.
LILY OF FRANCE CORSET CO. 303 SIXTH AVE, NEW YORK

SEND FOR FREE
DE LUXE
STYLE CATALOGUE

McCallum SILK HOSIERY

"You just know she wears them"

WHEN you wear McCallum Silk Stockings
there comes that little extra thrill of wearing the
recognized best.

Nowhere will you find as many styles and
designs in silk stockings as you will
find in McCallum. There are plain
ones for every-day wear, clocked
models for sports wear, exquisite
sheer ones for formal occasions.

Among the most popular numbers are 105—
113—122—199 in black, and 152—153—199 in
colors. A copy of our illustrated catalogue showing a great many McCallum models will be sent
to you free upon request.

Every shop does not carry
McCallum Silk Stockings, but
those that have the loveliest
things do.

McCallum
Silk Hosiery

CAMMEYER
Branch De Luxe
677 Fifth Avenue
New York

Exclusive Footwear for Women

Tom Wye

WOMEN are learning that
the secret of appearing
smartly turned-out on the beach
lies in the selection of one of
the new Tom Wye Swimming
Suits. They can be had in
two-piece or California style
garments made of our specially
knit material, in all the season's
most wanted shades.

We will gladly send you the
name of the nearest merchant
who can supply you.

TOM WYE, Inc., Winchendon, Mass.

Women to whom smartness of design is as important as dainty luxury of fabric highly prize "Niagara Maid" UNDERWEAR of silk

D ISTINCTION in style, combined with simplicity, is not easy to attain. Real art in designing and skill in tailoring make this combination possible. A slant pocket style, universally liked.

THE WAYNE

DEPEND ON KUPPENHEIMER VALUE

Kuppenheimer merchants are now showing suits of TIGERTWIST, TROJAN WEAVE and CASTILIANS-original in pattern and color-the ranking fabrics from the world's looms. Created to give you fine style and extra value-just as FAMOUS FIFTIES set the '50 standard.

Fur Collar Coat. There comes a time when a man owes himself a fur collar over-garment. The Kuppenheimer form-fitting overcoat with Hudson Seal collar, or the Blizzard Ulster with broad Beaver collar, is unquestionably good form for street wear, dress or motoring.

CLOTHES APPEARANCE IS important to your success—don't slight it—be judged by your clothes taste, Kuppenheimer good clothes.

You'll not only buy the best made clothes, but you'll buy the best clothes appearance. You never go wrong, any way, selecting Kuppenheimer clothes.

1144

The popular Double Breasted at its best—
in Hickey-Freeman Customized Clothes.

Interwoven Socks

REG. U.S. PAT. OFF

IN THE REALM OF
MODERN ACHIEVEMENT

JUDGE

1925

1146

CHAPTER 39

THE ROARING TWENTIES

Hardly had the Roaring Twenties ended when that flamboyant decade began to take on the aura of legend. Although the revolution in morals was its most sensational manifestation, other forces contributed equally to its special quality.

It was, for one thing, an age of unabashed materialism. Enormous paper profits were made not only by the large stock speculators but by the smallest investors; "playing the market" became a national pastime. By putting up a nominal sum, one could "buy on margin"—that is, hold stocks for only a small percentage of their total value. Thus the mechanic, the storekeeper, the salesman, and anyone else in the middle-income groups could participate with the dream of parlaying his down payment into big money. The extent to which the "little people" played the market encouraged

The flapper, with lipstick and rolled stockings, and the callow collegian, with hip flask, cigarette holder, and flashy roadster, were stock characters in the gallery of John Held, Jr., portraitist of the Jazz Age. Here they gaily greet the New Year of 1925 from the cover of Judge, *a humor magazine of the day.*

the formation of huge industrial and commercial empires, some of which, unfortunately, were supported by watered stock. When the market broke late in 1929, the whole structure tumbled like a house of cards. Instead of wiping out only a comparatively few professional gamblers, the crash ruined thousands of amateur "investors," many of whom had mortgaged everything they owned.

But as the market spiraled ever upward, and the boom continued unabated, few concerned themselves with any unhappy thoughts that the worst might happen. The easy-come, easy-go philosophy induced millions to fill their homes with every convenience available, and in answer to the demand, manufacturers turned out a mounting volume of radios, refrigerators, irons, toasters, vacuum cleaners, and washing machines. Everyone had to have an automobile—and better, two. To encourage sales, dealers began to make goods available "on time." Like the speculator who could buy his stock for a small amount down, the buyer of automobiles and home appliances had only to make a token payment to take his new acquisition out of the showroom. Now millions of Americans actually owned only 10% to 20% of each item they contracted for, and in this sense they, too, were buying on margin.

Enormous sums of money were also spent on entertainment—and in the 1920s there was no dearth of amusements. The jazz band with its wild, syncopated rhythms became as much a symbol of the era as the stock market, and in sedate ballrooms and speakeasies, in college fraternity houses and country clubs, millions danced to the rage of the moment—the fox trot, the lame duck, the grizzly bear, the black bottom, or, most famous of all, the Charleston. In the big cities, more lavish entertainment could be found in the theater "spectacles" staged by such enterprising showmen as Florenz Ziegfeld and Earl Carroll, who found it hugely profitable to "glorify" the American girl.

Of all popular art forms, however, the movies captured the fancy of the public most vividly. Not only were they still a novelty, but Hollywood producers had managed to gauge with

In the '20s, female hearts raced madly over Rudolph Valentino, an Italian immigrant gardener whom chance had made into a Great Lover in the guise of an actor.

1148

remarkable success the tempo of the times. Americans wanted something daring and bizarre, and that is what they got. One purveyor of celluloid excitement advertised his product with typical flamboyance: "Brilliant men, beautiful jazz babies, champagne baths, midnight revels, petting parties in the purple dawn." Rivals offered such enticements as *Sinners in Silk* and *Women Who Give.*

Sex appeal was the big drawing card. To the public, acting talent seemed to mean little (and it was hard to discern anyway, as the "talkies," which demanded something more than emotional overplaying, were not introduced until late in the decade). The leading cinematic sex symbol was Rudolph Valentino, an Italian immigrant gardener who could offer his public little more than long sideburns and a passionate Latin manner. Yet he was catapulted to international fame as a Great Lover in such vehicles as *The Sheik* and *The Four Horsemen of the Apocalypse.* He obviously heightened the heartbeat of women of all ages, for when he died in 1926, some 30,000 fans crowded around the New York mortician's where he lay in state, and a near-riot took place as they jostled one another for one last look. Before his body could be interred, Tin Pan Alley capitalized upon the event by turning out *There's a New Star in Heaven Tonight,* with Valentino on the sheet-music cover.

Sports competed with movies for public attention, and athletes, too, be-

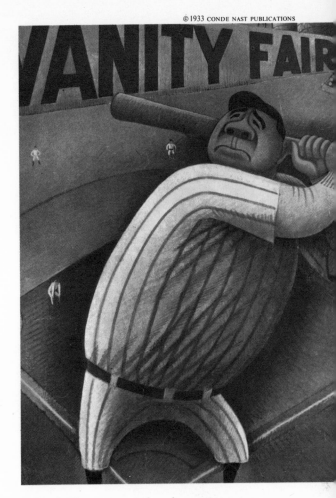

Babe Ruth, once a pitcher, became a great box-office attraction after he started hitting home runs for the Yankees. He was already a legend, two years before retirement, when he appeared on Vanity Fair.

came national idols. An Illinois youngster named Harold "Red" Grange brought college football to the fore with his Saturday afternoon touchdown rampages. When he quit school to join the professional Chicago Bears, he became such a drawing card that he received a salary which, one writer estimated, amounted to $1,000 for every

George Bellows painted Argentina's Luis Firpo, "Wild Bull of the Pampas," knocking Jack Dempsey out of the ring in 1923, but Dempsey came back to win.

minute he spent on the football field.

The rough-and-tumble of the grid-iron was closely rivaled by the violent action of the boxing ring. Here William Harrison "Jack" Dempsey was the undisputed king until 1926, when a former marine, Gene Tunney, uncrowned him one rainy September night in Philadelphia. The return bout, held in Chicago, attracted over 100,000 fight fans, who paid more than $2,500,000 to see Dempsey's unsuccessful comeback attempt. Millions more flocked to baseball parks, where a truly American game had be-come a big business. Here reigned George Herman "Babe" Ruth, the "Sultan of Swat," whose powerful swing netted him a record-breaking 60 home runs in one season (1927) and nearly $1,500,000 during his career, as well as another $500,000 from vaudeville appearances, commercial endorsements, and movies.

The "noble experiment"

When the doughboys came back, they found many changes; not the least was an absence of alcoholic beverages. The nation (much of which was already dry) had decided to abolish the saloon once and for all: Prohibition—the "noble experiment"—had come at last. "The country accepted it," Frederick Lewis Allen wrote, "not only willingly, but almost absent-mindedly." When the Eighteenth Amendment came before the Senate in 1917, it was passed by a one-sided vote after only 13 hours of debate. When the House of Representatives accepted it a few months later, the debate upon the amendment as a whole occupied only a single day. The state legislatures ratified it in short order; by January, 1919, some two months after the armistice, the necessary three-quarters of the states had fallen into line and the amendment was part of the Constitution. Officially, nationwide prohibition was supposed to take effect on January 16, 1920; actually, under the Wartime Prohibition Law, passed just before the armistice, it began in the summer of 1919.

A majority of Americans probably endorsed prohibition in the beginning, but the public rapidly grew disenchanted with it. The hip flask, filled with illicit, or "bootleg," whiskey and displayed openly and shamelessly, soon became another familiar symbol of the era. Every community of any size had its "speakeasies," where homemade and imported alcoholic beverages could be bought.

The speakeasies did a rushing business. Keeping them supplied was an occupation for many thousands of bootleggers, rumrunners, and beer barons, who were obliged to work beyond the pale of the law. Often their rivalries and differences of opinion resulted in open warfare and gangland slayings. Thanks to wartime technology, they had new and deadly weapons at their disposal—hand grenades (suitable for blowing up com-

A typical New York speakeasy entrance was under the stoop of a brownstone. The customers had to pass scrutiny to get in.

petitors' establishments), submachine guns, and fast boats and getaway cars.

The Eighteenth Amendment had a host of both defenders and detractors. The drys insisted it was a success, sharply reducing deaths, divorces, accidents, and poverty. But the wets held it was as senseless as the attempts to enforce it were futile. As one notorious figure of the era said, "They might as well have been trying to dry up the Atlantic with a post-office blotter." Franklin P. Adams, in his column in the New York *World,* expressed a similar view:

> *Prohibition is an awful flop.*
> *We like it.*
> *It can't stop what it's meant to stop.*
> *We like it.*
> *It's left a trail of graft and slime.*
> *It's filled our land with vice and crime,*
> *It can't prohibit worth a dime.*
> *Nevertheless, we're for it.*

In other words, those who wanted prohibition could say they had it; those who wanted to drink, drank. Thus, as a social experiment, prohibition proved an utter failure. Not only was it impossible to enforce, but in providing the underworld with its chief source of revenue, it fostered an evil far worse than the one it attempted to suppress. The American public, which had once willingly or at least resignedly accepted prohibition, gradually came to look upon it as the ill-advised measure it was. And yet, because the issue was considered political dynamite, the movement to abol-

ish prohibition made little headway during the '20s. Not until 1933, the first year of Franklin D. Roosevelt's administration, was it repealed.

"100% American"

The war years sharply stimulated American nationalism—a development that became more noticeable as the '20s wore on. It was part of a general pattern of suspicion and retreat that encouraged both commercial and domestic isolation, emphasized homegrown ideas and products, and blurred, if not blinded, the view of events abroad.

For one thing, this national myopia sharply affected immigration policies. Employers who once had welcomed the influx of cheap and docile foreign workers now became frightened by local labor unrest and by what appeared to be the spreading threat of a new and dangerously radical spirit in Europe. Old prejudices against foreigners were sharpened as the practice of blaming labor agitation upon the foreign-born became more common. Ironically, many liberals also joined the mounting clamor, claiming the influx of immigrant

The law sometimes caught up with those who broke it during prohibition. At the top, a shipload of smuggled liquor is seized by revenue agents; in the center, a group is searched for hip flasks; and at the bottom is the aftermath of a raid upon The House of Morgan, a speakeasy owned by top entertainer Helen Morgan.

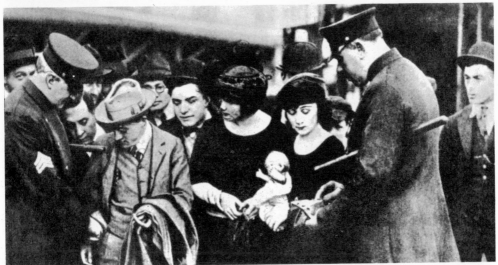

1153

workers was lowering both wages and labor's standard of living. There was a widespread feeling, too, that the newcomers—especially those from southern and eastern Europe—would corrupt not only the American political system but our "racial" stock as well.

Congress responded to these pressures by further tightening immigration laws. Under a law passed in May, 1921, quotas were imposed limiting the number of immigrants in any one year to 3% of the foreign-born of each nationality in the United States in 1910. The law was mainly aimed at immigrants from southern Europe, the bulk of whom had come to America after that year. But it did not cut back the number of new arrivals enough to suit the legislators, who, in 1924, passed an even more restrictive law, reducing the number admitted from 3% to 2% and basing the quota on the census of 1890. This resulted in diminishing the flow of foreign workers to a minute proportion of the American labor force.

Closely allied with antiforeign sentiment was a fear of radical activity, which at times verged on hysteria. In

A prohibition headquarters (top) in New Jersey of a huge liquor syndicate had bulletproof steel walls. The center photograph shows part of what was taken there after a raid. (Note short-wave radio.) At the bottom are victims of Chicago's Valentine's Day massacre, an episode in 1929's ruthless gang wars.

1919, especially, labor unrest was so widespread (in that year alone there were some 3,630 strikes involving over 4,000,000) that many felt a revolution was at hand. The organization of the Communist Party of America did little to ease nervous minds, even though its membership was microscopic. But the so-called "Red scare" rose to a height of frenzy when time bombs addressed to various leaders of business and government were discovered in post offices throughout the land. Only one exploded, blowing off the hands of a Georgia Senator's house servant.

A. Mitchell Palmer, Wilson's Attorney General, thereupon launched an anti-Red campaign that would, before it had run its course, prove the most serious infringement of civil liberties since the Sedition Act of John Adams' day. Although Congress refused to supply the Attorney General with a sedition act of his own, Palmer went ahead, arresting some 6,000 persons in a series of surprise raids on January 2, 1920. His purpose was to round up alien members of the Communist or Communist-Labor Parties, but many of those taken in were American citizens innocent of any connection with Communism. The whole procedure was so indiscriminate that in one New England city, those who attempted to visit the imprisoned were jailed on the theory that they, too, must be Communists. After a period of unjustified detention, about one-third of the catch was released; even-

*Still disputed are the trial and conviction of Nicola Sacco and Bartolomeo Van-
zetti (above) for the murder of a paymaster in 1920. Many thought them innocent.*

tually, some 500 aliens were deported.

Meanwhile, the Ku Klux Klan was causing thoughtful Americans concern. Founded during reconstruction, it was revived in the South during the '20s, mainly to guarantee a continuation of white supremacy. Soon, however, it spread across the land and found just as many adherents north of the Mason-Dixon line as south of it. In a catchall program that was anti-Semitic, anti-Catholic, antialien, and, of course, anti-Red, the Klan followed the pattern of its ancestor by putting on nocturnal parades of white-sheeted marchers who intimidated, flogged, and even killed some of those who incurred its displeasure. By the mid-'20s, the membership was reckoned at somewhere between 4,000,000 and 6,000,-000. After a series of lurid scandals involving some of the Klan's leaders, however, the organization fell into a quick decline, and by the end of the decade, the sinister power it once wielded had all but vanished.

Perhaps no event pointed up .the

The '20s saw the rebirth of the bigoted Ku Klux Klan, whose strength was so great for a few years that it could march without interference through Washington.

struggle between political reactionaries and liberals over the Red question more than the Sacco-Vanzetti case. In 1920, two Italian immigrants, Nicola Sacco and Bartolomeo Vanzetti, were arrested as suspects in the murder of a shoe-factory paymaster at South Braintree, Massachusetts. At the trial, in 1921, they were convicted and sentenced to death. To many, the real reason for the verdict was that the men were professed anarchists, immigrants, and pacifists, who had evaded the draft during the war.

There were protests from people of all shades of opinion in the United States, and even in Europe and Latin America there were demonstrations. The trial became an international *cause célèbre*. So great was the uproar that in July, 1927, six years after the trial, Governor Alvan T. Fuller of Massachusetts appointed a commission headed by President Abbott Lawrence Lowell of Harvard to investigate the case. It sustained the verdict, and a month later Sacco and Vanzetti were electrocuted. The out-

1157

Theatre, OCTOBER, 1927

Movie actress Clara Bow became famous only after novelist Elinor Glyn said she had the rare, indefinable quality—"It."

By 1928, 10,000,000 receivers were in use. This equaled the figure for all the rest of the world.

Early programs had their limitations, but before long the industry offered a wide range of listening. The day of setting-up exercises early in the morning, followed by recipes and then an extended period of dance music, soon gave way to more varied fare. In 1924, candidates of both political parties used the new medium to disseminate their programs and arguments, and for the first time Americans could sit in on a Presidential campaign.

Movies, of course, competed with radio for the attention of the public. In the more than 20,000 movie houses across the land, some 175,000 miles of film were shown each week to an estimated 100,000,000 customers. In 1927, the motion picture industry realized its dream of supplementing images with sound. When Al Jolson appeared in *The Jazz Singer* and actually sang to the patrons, a revolution took place in the movie world. The "talkie" did not win out over the silent film, however, without serious casualties. To the consternation of some producers, more than one virile hero of the silent screen turned out to have a far from robust voice on the synchronized recording that preceded the sound track.

cry of the intellectuals who had spoken for the condemned men reverberated into the next decade, a time of economic turmoil when radical political views did not seem so dangerous.

Culture for the masses

Despite the emphasis upon hip flasks and the ascending hemlines, outwardly giddy, gay America made some surprising (if sometimes dubious) cultural advances. The transmission of ideas was no longer through the printed word alone, but also through new media produced by the fast growth of technology. The radio, for example, was now available to the average home. By 1921, about $10,-000,000 worth of radio sets had been bought; within eight years, annual sales were well over $800,000,000.

Despite the growth of radio and the movies, the printed word still continued to command respect. The number of newspapers did decline sharply, ·

but this did not mean fewer readers. More than 2,000 newspapers disappeared between 1914 and 1929, most of them swallowed up by mergers. Magazines, on the other hand, showed large gains, from about 70,000,000 subscribers in 1914 to 111,000,000 in 1925.

A glance at the bookshelf of a home of the '20s—or more particularly the bookshelf of a summer cabin, where a lighter brand of reading was preferred—would have supported the notion that the public was in search of the sensational and bizarre. The predominant theme of many new books seemed to be sex. The trend began at the turn of the decade, when such gifted realistic writers as Sherwood Anderson, John Dos Passos, and Theodore Dreiser chose not to shy away from subjects that hitherto had been forbidden. But soon opportunists appeared who dropped all pretense of art and simply emphasized sex for its own sake. Commenting on the works of Elinor Glyn, a novelist of this period, Mark Sullivan stated, "All her books were utterly worthless, and all were tremendously popular." Mrs. Glyn made one doubtful contribution to the English language when she transformed the simple pronoun "it" into a symbol of sex appeal. Clara Bow, a popular movie star of the day, was publicized as the "It Girl," making millions of her admirers wish that they, too, had "It."

Fortunately, American writers were also concerning themselves with seri-

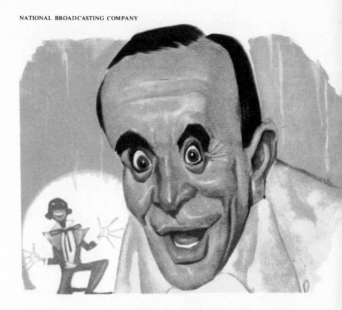

Al Jolson was a great musical comedy star when he gambled his reputation on the first talking movie, The Jazz Singer.

ous themes, not the least of which was a searching criticism of their own society. In deeply satiric novels like *Main Street* (1920) and *Babbitt* (1922), Sinclair Lewis attacked the smug world of the small-town businessman. Ironically, the Pulitzer Prize committee, in choosing Lewis' *Arrowsmith* (1925), found that it portrayed the "wholesome atmosphere of American life." Few in the Jazz Age seemed offended by the angry author's denunciation of the current moral standards, or the shabbiness of the businessman's motives, or the crass material aspirations of a representative American small town in a boom era.

No single figure personified the times more than F. Scott Fitzgerald. His own life in many ways represented the carefree, hard-drinking,

Chronicler of the Jazz Age, F. Scott Fitz-gerald poses lightheartedly with wife Zelda and daughter Frances in Paris in 1925.

Sinclair Lewis—bitter satirist of his coun-try's most revered institutions—is carica-tured as throttling the American eagle.

partygoing ideal of many cynical young Americans. Two of his books, *This Side of Paradise* (1920) and *The Beautiful and Damned* (1922), pictured the efforts of the college and young married sets to conceal their sense of insecurity by displays of gaiety. Much better than either of these was *The Great Gatsby* (1925). Although in it Fitzgerald still dealt with the social antics and alcoholism of the gay rich, he tried to probe problems of Ameri-can life and, in doing so, showed that he had real creative talent.

Cynicism and futility pervaded

other postwar novels. John Dos Passos, a wartime ambulance driver, expressed them in *Three Soldiers* (1921) and *Manhattan Transfer* (1925). In a larger work, the trilogy *U.S.A.,* he presented a panoramic view of America in the '20s that was notable for its bitterness. Ernest Hemingway was another of those who returned home from World War I to write of his generation's disillusion with the Great Crusade. As the hero of his famous war novel *A Farewell to Arms* (1929) put it, "I was embarrassed by the words sacred, glorious, and sacri-

The rugged American was the character Ernest Hemingway portrayed in his novels and assumed for himself in his private life.

John Dos Passos, at 25, wrote Three Soldiers, *his first success, out of the cynicism and futility of his war years.*

fice and the expression in vain. We had heard them, sometimes standing in rain almost out of earshot, so that only the shouted words came through, and had read them, on proclamations, now for a long time, and I had seen nothing sacred, and the things that were glorious had no glory and the sacrifices were like the stockyards in Chicago, if nothing was done with the meat except to bury it . . . Abstract words such as glory, honor, courage, were obscene."

The "gay decade," so fondly remembered by later generations, was a strange mixture of calm and conflict. For many, it was the most prosperous time they had ever known, and the ease with which money was made generated an optimism that produced reckless economic thinking and extreme political conservatism. On the other hand, the social behavior of Americans could truly be characterized by the word "revolt." The '20s were 10 years of materialism, ultra-nationalism, isolationism, great prosperity, and declining morality—and yet out of them came a number of the century's significant literary works.

MAIN TEXT CONTINUES IN VOLUME 14

Henry Ford: A Complex Man

A SPECIAL CONTRIBUTION BY

ALLAN NEVINS

He built two legends in his lifetime —one about his Model T and another about himself—and he is still one of the most elusive figures in the story of 20th-century America.

One of the most remarkable facts about Henry Ford is that his fame and the Ford legend were born almost simultaneously. He was tossed into international eminence on January 5, 1914, when the Ford Motor Company startled the globe by announcing the incredible minimum wage of $5 a day.

Until then, Henry Ford had touched the national consciousness only glancingly. He had founded the Ford Motor Company in 1903, when already 40; after some years of uncertain struggle, he had produced a model, distinguished from previous Models B, N, and S by the letter T, which precisely filled a ravenous national want; he had erected at Highland Park, just outside Detroit, one of the most efficient factories in the world. He and a group of tireless, gifted associates were developing that implement of global change termed mass production—still little understood (for most people equate it with quantity production, which is merely one of its half-dozen chief components), and then not under-

In this portrait of Henry Ford, painted after he had achieved his success, the lean, eager features suggest his strong emotions and ideas.

stood at all. Ford was, of course, known in the Detroit area as an astonishingly successful manufacturer, but elsewhere until 1914 the name Ford connoted a brand, not a man. Before then, facts on his mind and character are scanty and give no real portrait. But after 1914 the spate of articles, books, and reminiscences becomes torrential. "The Ford and Charlie Chaplin," remarked Will Rogers, "are the best known objects in the world." As the renown grew, unfortunately, so did the confusing legend. As one parodist of the Ford Motor Company slogan put it, "Watch the Ford myths go by!"

Lord Northcliffe, the English publisher, extolled Henry Ford to the British public as a great American. For a time in 1923–24, Ford's quasi-autobiography, translated as *Mein Leben und Werke,* was one of the two best-selling books in Germany. From Sweden to Turkey a new word, *Fordismus,* epitomized the new mass-production engineering, the low-price economy of abundance, and the efficiency speed-up. Throughout Latin America, Ford's personality seemed to sum up American traits. In Russia, painfully aware of her industrial backwardness, Henry Ford was a figure about whom *moujiks* and mechanics dreamed.

In the United States, too, the Ford of fact and the Ford of myth were for a time indistinguishably blended.

Between 1914–29, American masses took Ford to their hearts; every clerk and farmer had his own image of the man. The task of gaining a true portrait was complicated by writers who tried to establish an artificial pattern, and by Ford himself, who began issuing pronunciamentos and essays in self-portraiture that wove Oriental embroideries about the real man.

At once the most impressive and disturbing fact about Henry Ford is the extent to which he held up a mirror to the modern American character. His technological talents, his feats as an organizer, his individualistic economies, his social blindness, his frequent brilliant insights, his broad veins of ignorance, prejudice, and suspicion at first glance seem unique. But his labyrinthine complications were not different to that degree. For in strength and weakness, pioneering thrust and reactionary conservatism, generosity and selfishness he came near typifying the America of his time.

What made him a tremendous American force was his clear perception of five fundamental facts—that the American people wanted and needed cars in millions; that a single durable, inexpensive model could meet that demand; that new technological elements (precise standardization of parts, the multiplication and perfection of machine tools, separation of the job into minutely specialized functions, quantity manufacture, continuous motion, Taylor time studies) could supply the millions of cheap vehicles; that steady price reduction meant steady market expansion ("Every time I lower the price a dollar we gain a thousand new buyers"); and that high wages meant high buying power.

All this was obvious, when demonstrated. Until demonstrated, it was so far from patent that the ablest manufacturers scoffed, and Ford had to battle his principal partner and the trend of the times to prove it.

Next to this insight, Henry Ford's most striking gift was his peculiar engineering talent. As a few rare men are born with the power of instantaneously performing intricate mathematical computations, he had the power of divining almost any mechanism at a glance. He *read* engines. Indeed, one associate says that the great engine collections Ford made were his historical library. "They were living things to him, those machines. He could al-

Ford admired Thomas Edison and went with him and tireman Harvey Firestone on camping trips. Left to right: Edison, naturalist John Burroughs, Ford, and Firestone.

*On his third attempt at automobile manufacturing, Ford came up with this 1903
Model A runabout. It had two speeds, eight horsepower, and sold for $750.*

most diagnose the arrangement by touching
it." That gift had been with him when as a
boy he took apart and reassembled every
watch he could reach, and spent a Sunday
afternoon, his father away, in disassembling
and restoring much of a steam engine.

Another significant trait was Ford's remarkable capacity for sustained work.
The relaxed air that the mature Henry Ford
wore in public, together with his well-
advertised recreation in square dancing, col-
lecting Americana, and making excursions
with Thomas Edison, Harvey Firestone, and
John Burroughs, concealed the fact that
from boyhood on, he led a singularly labori-
ous, concentrated life. In his prime, his
frequent periods of intense industry would
have exhausted a less resilient man. At
Highland Park and River Rouge his responsibilities were always enormous. But his
engineering passion made one important
part of them—the responsibility for steady
mechanical experiment—almost a refreshment.

Day-to-day study of his activities reveals a
man in whose quick brain exploded a steady
succession of technological ideas. Writes an
associate, "One time he was up at Harbor
Beach, where he had a summer cottage, and
he was coming home with his son Edsel.
Suddenly he said, 'I've got the idea. We're
going to put a worm drive on the tractor.' "
That idea solved the vexatious problem of
power transmission to the rear axle—or so he
hoped; and he drove his tractor factory ahead
with enhanced zest.

In experimentation, pioneering, the quest
of fruitful mechanical innovations, Henry
Ford at his apogee was happiest. In 1914-15,
he became interested in making a better electric car, and reports spread that he and Edison
were collaborating. If the idea proved good
(which it did not), he thought of forming a
separate company. A later scheme called for
the use of plastics in building cars; in fact, a
plastic-body car *was* built.

Ford's technological genius was one aspect
of a mind peculiar for its intuitive nature.
Ford hit upon truths by divination, not rati-
ocination. His aides credited him with what

biographer Dean Marquis termed a "supernormal perceptive faculty." Marquis called him "a dreamer," adding that he had a different view from other men of what was possible and impossible. "I suppose the reason is that men who dream walk by faith, and faith laughs at mountains."

Reliance on intuition partly explains why Ford was so amazingly unpredictable. It also partly explains the crippling isolation of his mind, for a brain that cannot be reasoned with cannot be penetrated. Until 1914, he was open to the counsel of certain men—his partners Alex Malcomson and John S. Gray, his indispensable business manager James Couzens, the brilliant designer Harold Wills, and others. Later, he placed himself beyond advice. His mental isolation "is about as perfect as he can make it," wrote Marquis as early as 1923. His capable production chief, Charles E. Sorensen, who ought to know, believes that Ford had only two lifelong friends—Sorensen himself, and the strong head of his British company, Percival L. D. Perry.

The dreamer, the man of intuitive mind, is usually an artist, and many puzzling contradictions, even many repugnant acts in Ford become comprehensible if we think of him as essentially a man of artistic temperament. His detachment, his arch, wry humor, his constant self-projection into the spotlight, his ability to lift himself above business minutiae, his readiness to do some terrible things with as little seeming consciousness of their quality as Byron or Swift showed in *their* misdeeds—all suggest an artistic bent. The Model T was homely awkwardness itself, but it had artistic elements. Highland Park was the most artistic factory built in America in its day. And what of the aesthetic element in the old dances, old folk songs, old buildings, and old machines Ford loved so well?

Above all, he had the artist's desire to remake the world after his own pattern. His gospel of abundant work, high wages, and low prices; his plans for decentralizing industry to combine it with rural life and rural virtues; his enthusiastic forays into "better"

Ford had a mischievous sense of humor. Here, on an outing, he plays the dour Western badman.

agriculture, education, and recreation were an artist's effort to impose his own vision on life.

There was also a complex enmity between Ford the artist and Ford the untutored countryman whose parents had been Michigan pioneers, and whose own formal education was limited to a few years in a very common school. This conflict twisted the whole skein of his character. An artist needs a cultivated background; Henry Ford's background was that of Anglo-Irish tenant farmers. Though his homely early environment had advantages, its limitations always fettered him.

Henry Ford always remained a countryman in his plain way of living. When his fortune first grew, he said plaintively that the chief difference in his way of life was that "Mrs. Ford no longer does the cooking"—and he preferred her cookery. His puritanic condemnation of smoking, drinking, and marital

1166

irregularities conformed to the principles described in Thorstein Veblen's essay *The Country Town*. He was a countryman also in his devotion to work as a virtue in itself. His cure for nearly all ills was more work.

True to the frontiersman's instinct, he preferred trial and error to precise planning. Contemptuous of elaborate record-keeping, he once made a bonfire of forms used to keep track of spare parts. Hostile to meticulous organization, he ran even the huge Highland Park plant without formal titles or administrative grades. He long derided careful cost accounting. In this, thinks one surviving executive, he was right. Success in the automotive industry at first depended not on computation of costs to the third decimal point, but on courageous innovations in design and engineering and on the acceptability of models and prices to the public. Ford stayed in the field of bold experiment; cost accounting might have hampered him.

He also had the frontiersman's intense hatred of monopoly and special privilege. To be sure, he long enjoyed a practical monopoly of the low-priced car, but he could say that he achieved it without favor and without warring on any competitor. His dislike of patents, his course in throwing open to public view and general use Ford machines and methods—all harmonized with the frontier attitude.

Much more might be said on the pleasanter inheritances from the rural environment—his rather appealing inarticulateness; his dislike of class lines; his warm love of nature, and the feeling for wild life that made him build shelters for rabbits, grow corn for crows, and keep warm water available all winter in the hope of retaining migratory songbirds in the North. One of the most important parts of his countryman's heritage was his stubborn originality of thought—when he did think. He did not take ideas secondhand, but hammered them out for himself, usually on walks in field and wood. Often the ideas were immature. But sometimes he came up with a concept startling for its novel glint of truth.

Like other untutored men, he had a deep suspicion of the uncomprehended, a strong inclination to prejudice, and susceptibility to bad counsel. His antagonism to Wall Street was largely simple distrust of what he did not understand. It is significant that his suspiciousness grew marked when he came under fire. He thought that some newspapers had begun to hound him when he announced the $5 day, and others when he battled for peace and the League of Nations.

"A good part of the American press, not all, is not free," he told reporters. "They misquoted me, distorted what I said, made up lies." The malicious attitude of part of the press toward Ford's Peace Ship, the aspersions on his motives in lifting wages from $2.25 to $5 a day, the attacks on his son Edsel as an alleged draft-dodger, the storm of ridicule accompanying his Senatorial campaign and his libel suit against the Chicago *Tribune* (which he won, with an award of 6¢ in damages) were indeed outrageous. Because Ford was a sensitive man, they converted his early idealism into cynicism. Had he had more education, poise, and perspective, he would not only have avoided some of the occasions for ridicule; he would have met ridicule with a heavier armor.

Out of his sense of needing an agency for

Henry Ford and his son Edsel stand in front of the 10,000,000th car, produced in 1924.

defense and for stating his ideas came the Dearborn *Independent*. Out of his ignorance and suspiciousness came the lamentable anti-Semitic campaign of that weekly, for which he apologized only after vast harm had been done. In this unhappy crusade he had collaborators. E. G. Pipp, who resigned as editor rather than share in it, frankly said to Ford's spokesman, W. J. Cameron, "You are furnishing the brains, Ford the money, and E. G. Liebold the prejudices." Cameron and Liebold furnished some of the methods, too, but as Liebold says, "As long as Mr. Ford wanted it done, it was done." The responsibility was Ford's. That he had no deep-seated race prejudices, but really believed in a fictitious bogy called the International Jew, does not palliate his offense. This, like the shortsighted harshness toward labor organizations, was the abortion of an uninformed mind and uncultivated spirit.

Some aspects of the man remain wholly inexplicable. Highly diffident in some ways, he had an irrepressible desire to be oracular about topics of which he knew nothing. Kindly in most personal relations, he nevertheless countenanced such cruel treatment of subordinates as the smashing of their desks in token of discharge. At times he indulged a good-humored liking for horseplay; at other times he was sternly unapproachable. Sharply practical, he yet cherished some curious superstitions. A churchgoing Episcopalian, he leaned strongly to an unorthodox belief in metempsychosis, or transmigration of souls. There was always something in him of an urchin—a wry, cross-grained, brilliant adolescent.

Yet in this fascinating personality, we come back always to the image of the artist. Much that is otherwise puzzling becomes comprehensible if we think of him in that way—struggling, despite many limitations and handicaps, to remake his world a little nearer to the heart's desire. He wanted to abolish war ("a habit, and a filthy habit," he said), and thus the great gesture of the Peace Ship. He wanted to exclude drink, class divisions, idleness, and disorder. He wanted to get rid of money as

anything but a part of the mechanism of production—"part of the assembly line," or "the connecting rod."

Perhaps his poignant failure lay in his relationship to his son, to whom he gave both intense devotion and total incomprehension. Edsel was a man of the finest qualities of character and mind—upright, idealistic, public-spirited, and hard-working. He was highly philanthropic. In the factory, he got on well with others. In the world at large, he had a broader vision than his father. Some of Henry Ford's acts, such as the anti-Jewish campaign, grieved Edsel greatly, though he was too loyal to speak out publicly. Yet the father, while justly proud of him, committed a fundamental error: He tried to make Edsel in his own image. Of course, he failed in his effort, with anguish to both himself and his son. But the attempt was again, in part, an expression of the artist's desire to make the world over to suit his own vision.

As the years pass and we gain perspective, the blunders and misdeeds in Henry Ford's record will arouse less interest. His social primitivism will seem more a part of the general ignorance and gullibility of our adolescent American civilization. His great achievement will loom up as the significant fact of his career. By his labors in bringing mass production to birth, by his gospel of high production, low prices, and large consumption, he became the key figure in a far-reaching revolution. This fumbling artist actually did remold the world according to his vision. Talking with Edsel one day, he said of his great company: "We'll build this as well as we know how, and if we don't use it, somebody will use it. Anything that is good enough will be used." Of few of the industrial path-hewers of his time can it be said that they produced so much that is permanently and profitably usable.

Allan Nevins, eminent American historian, has won two Pulitzer Prizes, for his studies of Grover Cleveland and Hamilton Fish. Now senior research associate at the Huntington Library in California, he is also chairman of the editorial board of American Heritage *magazine.*

FOR FURTHER READING

Adams, Samuel Hopkins. *Incredible Era: The Life and Times of Warren Gamaliel Harding*. Boston: Houghton Mifflin, 1939. A newspaperman's biography, based mostly on information gathered from people who knew Harding personally.

Allen, Frederick Lewis. *Only Yesterday*. New York: Harpers, 1931. A lively social panorama of the Roaring Twenties.

Bailey, Thomas Aldrich. *Woodrow Wilson and the Great Betrayal*. New York: Macmillan, 1945. Wilson's struggles in trying to push the peace treaty through the Senate.

Commager, Henry Steele. *The American Mind*. New Haven: Yale University Press, 1950. An intellectual history of America from 1880 to 1950.

Dos Passos, John. *Mr. Wilson's War*. New York: Doubleday, 1962. An intimate portrait of the wartime President.

Falls, Cyril: *The Great War*. New York: Putnam, 1951. An admirable summary of World War I by a leading British military historian.

Faulkner, Harold Underwood. *From Versailles to the New Deal*. New Haven: Yale University Press, 1950. Chapter 9 discusses the particular problems of the farmer and the laborer in the '20s.

Fleming, Denna Frank. *The United States and the League of Nations, 1918–1920*. New York: Putnam, 1932. An examination of American attitudes toward joining a world community in the years following World War I.

Fuess, Claude M. *Calvin Coolidge, The Man from Vermont*. Boston: Little, Brown, 1940. The best of Coolidge biographies—strongly sympathetic.

Laidler, Harry W. and H. S. Rauschenbush. *Power Control*. New York: New Republic, 1928. A brief attack upon monopolistic practices in the power industry.

Leuchtenberg, William E. *The Perils of Prosperity, 1914–1932*. Chicago: University of Chicago Press, 1958. Brief and readable history of the United States from World War I to the depression, with an excellent bibliography.

Sann, Paul. *The Lawless Decade*. New York: Crown, 1957. A pictorial history of the transition from the prosperous 1920s to the New Deal.

Schriftgiesser, Karl. *This Was Normalcy*. Boston: Little, Brown, 1948. An often biting account of the years of Republican rule from 1920 to 1932.

Shideler, James H. *Farm Crisis, 1919–1923*. Berkeley: University of California Press, 1957. Describes agricultural problems in the years following World War I.

Slosson, Preston W. *The Great Crusade and After, 1914–1928*. New York: Macmillan, 1930. An intellectual and social history of these crucial years.

Soule, George. *Prosperity Decade: From the War to Depression: 1917–1929*. New York: Rinehart, 1947. A general economic history of the '20s.

Stallings, Laurence. *The Doughboys*. New York: Harper & Row, 1963. An ex-doughboy takes a fond look, after 45 years, at the war he fought in.

Wallace, Henry A. *New Frontiers*. New York: Reynal & Hitchcock, 1934. A discussion of agricultural problems by the New Deal Secretary of Agriculture.

THE AMERICAN HERITAGE NEW ILLUSTRATED HISTORY OF THE UNITED STATES

PUBLISHED BY DELL PUBLISHING CO., INC.

George T. Delacorte, Jr., *Publisher*   Helen Meyer, *President*
William F. Callahan, Jr., *Executive Vice-President*

Walter B. J. Mitchell, Jr., *Project Director;* Ross Claiborne, *Editorial Consultant;* William O'Gorman, *Editorial Assistant;* John Van Zwienen, *Art Consultant;* Rosalie Barrow, *Production Manager*

CREATED AND DESIGNED BY THE EDITORS OF AMERICAN HERITAGE MAGAZINE

James Parton, *Publisher;* Joseph J. Thorndike, Jr., *Editorial Director;* Bruce Catton, *Senior Editor;* Oliver Jensen, *Editor;* Richard M. Ketchum, *Editor, Book Division;* Irwin Glusker, *Art Director*

ROBERT R. ENDICOTT, *Project Editor-in-Chief*

James Kraft, *Assistant Editor;* Nina Page, Evelyn H. Register, Lynn Marett, *Editorial Assistants;* Lina Mainiero, *Copy Editor;* Murray Belsky, *Art Director;* Eleanor A. Dye, *Designer;* John Conley, *Assistant*

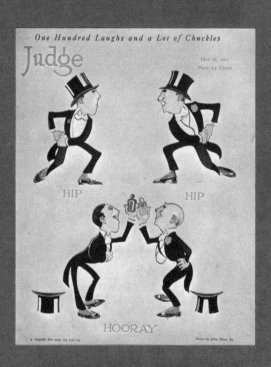

One Hundred Laughs and a Lot of Chuckles

Judge

HIP   HIP

HOORAY

IF YOU CAN'T TELL THE WORLD
SHE'S A GOOD LITTLE GIRL,
JUST SAY NOTHING AT ALL

Lyric by Al. Dubin and Irving Kahal   Music by Sammy Fain

BENNY MEROFF
SLAVE of JAZZ
AND HIS TWENTY FIVE PEPSTERS

Those DRAF-TIN' BLUES

Words & Music by
MACEO PINKARD

GRIFFIN
MUSIC
HOUSE
CHICAGO

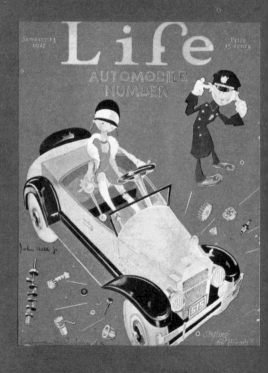

Life
AUTOMOBILE
NUMBER